The Big Book of Theme Parties, Snacks and Games

Compiled by Linda Bossoletti

This book contains decorating ideas, clip art, games and snacks for the following theme parties:
- International • Farm/Country • Bible Times • Mountain/Camping
- Pioneer/Western • Safari • Tropical Island • Hot Air Ballooning

Gospel Light

How to make clean copies from this book

You may make copies of portions of this book with a clean conscience if:

- ✦ you (or someone in your organization) are the original purchaser;
- ✦ you are using the copies you make for a noncommercial purpose (such as teaching or promoting a ministry) within your church or organization;
- ✦ you follow the instructions provided in this book.

However, it is ILLEGAL for you to make copies if:

- ✦ you are using the material to promote, advertise or sell a product or service other than for ministry fund-raising;
- ✦ you are using the material in or on a product for sale;
- ✦ you or your organization are **not** the original purchaser of this book.

By following these guidelines you help us keep our products affordable. Thank you.

Gospel Light

Publisher, William T. Greig
Senior Consulting Publisher, Dr. Elmer L. Towns
Publisher, Research, Planning and Development, Billie Baptiste
Senior Editor, Christy Weir
Senior Consulting Editors, Dr. Gary S. Greig, Wesley Haystead, M.S.Ed.
Editor, Theological and Biblical Issues, Bayard Taylor, M.Div.
Associate Editor, Kim Sullivan
Associate Technical Editor, Linda Mattia
Assistant Editor, Kathleen McIntosh
Assistant Editor, Linda Bossoletti
Senior Designer, Lori Hamilton

Contents

Contents

Cooking with Kids

The recipes and procedures in this book are designed to be used in small groups of one to six children so that each child can actively participate. There are sandwiches, snacks, salads, drinks and desserts. We hope these recipes will provide you and your children with many enjoyable learning experiences.

When planning to cook, preparation and organization are very important. Before you try recipes that require extensive measuring it's wise to provide several measuring experiences, showing the children the correct way to use both dry and liquid measuring utensils.

- Provide a comfortable working space that is child-sized;
- Gather and set out ingredients and equipment before children begin;
- Read through the recipe together;
- Go over safety rules together;
- Clean up as you go along.

Table Setting Ideas

- Make and decorate paper placemats. Paste pictures of theme ideas on the placemats.
- Make name cards.
- Create a theme centerpiece.

Safety and Health

- Always wash hands before handling food.
- Things that are hot don't always look hot. If someone gets burned, immediately hold the burned area under cold running water.
- When chopping, cutting or peeling food, use a cutting board.
- Keep pot handles on the stove turned away from you.
- Turn the burner or oven off before removing pans.
- Stand mixing bowls in the sink as you stir to avoid splashes.
- Use hand beaters, a large spoon, or a wire whip instead of electric beaters. This way, children have a chance to get the feel of the batter.
- Demonstrate and let children practice using utensils.
- Store sharp utensils out of children's reach.
- Keep hands dry while working in the kitchen. Wet, slippery hands can cause spills and accidents.
- Keep pot holders dry. If damp, they will absorb heat and lead to burns.
- When cutting with a knife, always cut away from yourself and keep fingers away from the blade.
- To help prevent steam burns, tip the lid away from you whenever you raise the cover of a hot pan.
- Electrical appliances should be used by ADULTS ONLY.
- Young children should not use the stove at all.
- Make sure hot foods are thoroughly cooked and any leftovers are quickly refrigerated.
- Instruct children in advance how to deal with a sneeze or a cough.

International

Theme craft ideas can be found in the
Celebrating Our Families — Crafts for Kids book,
available from Gospel Light.

International Decorations

Create an international marketplace by making a booth for each country represented. In each booth display travel posters, flags, maps and artifacts of the country represented.

Offer the sounds of each country by playing music on a cassette player at each booth. Introduce some tastes of each country by placing samples of foods and drinks at each booth. The host or hostess at each booth dresses in the traditional costume of the country represented.

You can use the clip art in this book to create bulletin board displays, country brochures or simple language guides. The clip art can also be enlarged to make life-sized wall decorations.

For instance, a booth of Japan might include:

- Travel posters of Japan
- Japanese flag
- Map of Japan
- Japanese fans
- Rice balls, green tea and honeyballs to sample
- Bonsai tree, Japanese art and table service
- Hostess dressed in a Kimono
- Japanese words of greeting
- Enlarged clip art of Japanese kites
- Japanese music playing on cassette recorder

International Clip Art

The Big Book of Theme Parties, Snacks and Games © 1997 by Gospel Light. Permission to photocopy granted.

Hello! – U.S.A.
Jambo! – Kenya
Guten Tag! – Germany
Priviet! – Russia
Cheerio! – England
Hola! – Mexico
Ciáo! – Italy
Bon Jour! – France
Top O' the Morning! – Ireland
G'day! – Australia
Konnichiwa! – Japan

Friendly Dog Salad

Materials Checklist

☐ forks

☐ kitchen scissors

☐ teaspoon

☐ paper towels

☐ 6 bowls

For each child—

☐ 1 lettuce leaf

☐ 1 canned pear half

☐ 1 canned prune

☐ 2 canned mandarin orange segments

☐ 1 maraschino cherry

☐ 1 raisin

☐ salad plate

    Makes 1 salad.

Preparation: Prepare one Friendly Dog Salad in advance for demonstration. Set out all materials so children can see ingredients. Have children wash and dry hands. Place lettuce leaves, pear halves, prunes, mandarin orange segments, maraschino cherries and raisins in bowls.

Procedure: Have each child wash lettuce leaf and pat dry with towel. Place on salad plate. Place the pear half cut side down on the lettuce leaf. Cut the prune lengthwise in half with scissors and take out pit. Place one of the prune halves at the large end of the pear half for the ear. (Eat the other prune half!) Use teaspoon to scoop out a tiny hole in the pear for the eye. Place raisin in the hole. Cut the maraschino cherry in half with the scissors. Place one half at the top of the narrow end of the pear for the nose. (Eat the other cherry half!) Use the mandarin orange segments for the collar.

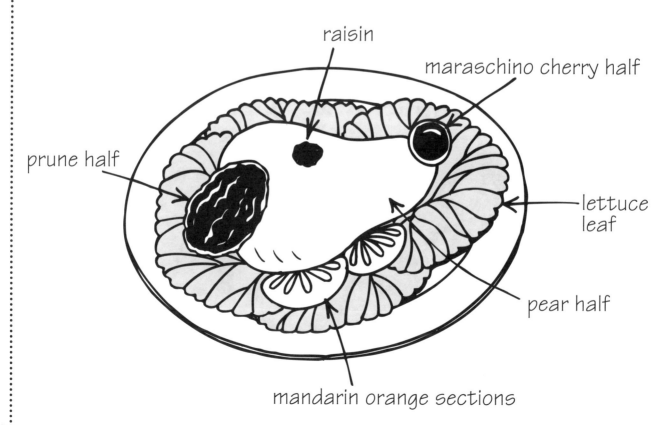

raisin

maraschino cherry half

prune half

lettuce leaf

pear half

mandarin orange sections

Lil' Pizzas

Materials Checklist

☐ 6 English muffins

☐ 1 (14 oz.) jar of pizza sauce

☐ 1 (8 oz.) pkg. of shredded mozzarella cheese

☐ bowls

☐ forks or knives

☐ spoons

☐ cookie sheet

☐ napkins

Optional (toppings)—

☐ small slices of salami, pepperoni or ham

☐ canned or fresh mushrooms and/or olives

Serves 12.

Preparation: Set out all materials so children can see ingredients. Place pizza sauce, cheese and toppings in bowls. Have children wash and dry hands.

Procedure: Heat the oven to 400°. Children use forks or knives to separate muffins in half. Use spoon to spread the cut side of each muffin half with a thin layer of the pizza sauce. Sprinkle cheese over sauce. Put muffins on cookie sheet. Bake until cheese melts. Serve hot. (*Optional:* Place small pieces of salami, pepperoni, ham, mushrooms or olives on top of the cheese before you put the pizzas in the oven.)

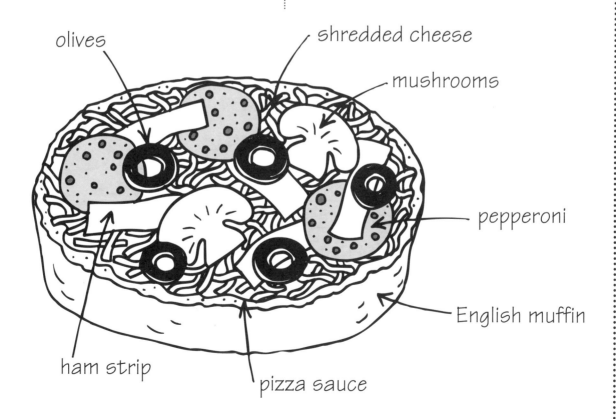

olives — shredded cheese — mushrooms — pepperoni — English muffin — ham strip — pizza sauce

Nana 'n' Cookie Pudding

Materials Checklist

☐ 6 ripe bananas

☐ 2 (6-oz.) pkgs. vanilla instant pudding

☐ milk

☐ 1 (12-oz.) box vanilla wafers

☐ 1 (8-oz.) container of thawed nondairy dessert topping (such as Cool Whip)

☐ 1 (7 oz.) pkg. flaked coconut

☐ rolling pin

☐ mixing bowl

☐ mixing spoon

☐ resealable plastic bags

☐ measuring cup

☐ knives

For each child—

☐ clear plastic cup

☐ spoon

Serves 10-12.

Preparation: Set out all materials so children can see ingredients. Place several cookies in each plastic bag. Have children wash and dry hands.

Procedure: Children peel and cut bananas into slices. Children make pudding according to package directions. Let stand five minutes. Next, using rolling pin, children take turns crushing wafers in plastic bags and place layer of crushed cookies into bottom of individual cups. Next, they spoon some of the pudding over the wafers and arrange banana slices over the pudding. Top with dessert topping and shredded coconut.

coconut

nondairy topping

bananas

pudding

cookie crumbs

Almond Cakes

Materials Checklist

- ☐ 1 c. shortening
- ☐ 1 c. sugar
- ☐ 1 beaten egg
- ☐ 3 c. flour
- ☐ 1½ tsp. baking soda
- ☐ 3 tsp. almond extract
- ☐ 4 Tbs. honey
- ☐ 36 almonds
- ☐ mixing bowl
- ☐ mixing spoon
- ☐ measuring cups
- ☐ measuring spoons
- ☐ cookie sheets
- ☐ napkins

Optional—
- ☐ chopsticks for children to experiment with
- ☐ red food coloring

Makes 3 dozen cookies.

Preparation: Set out all materials so children can see ingredients. Beat egg and grease cookie sheets with some shortening. Have children wash and dry hands.

Procedure: Preheat oven to 375°. Cream together shortening and sugar. Add beaten egg, then flour, baking soda, almond extract and honey. Blend well. Using hands, form dough into small (1-inch) balls, place two inches apart on cookie sheet, flatten with finger, and place an almond in center. (*Optional:* Put a few drops of red food coloring into a measuring cup, dip end of chopstick in it and place a red dot in the center of each cake. Omit almond.) Bake for 15 minutes.

almond

Soft Pretzels

Materials Checklist

- ☐ 1½ c. warm water
- ☐ 1 pkg. yeast
- ☐ 1 tsp. salt
- ☐ 1 Tbs. sugar
- ☐ 4 c. flour
- ☐ 1 beaten egg
- ☐ shortening
- ☐ pastry brush
- ☐ coarse salt
- ☐ measuring cups
- ☐ measuring spoon
- ☐ large mixing bowl
- ☐ mixing spoon
- ☐ cookie sheets
- ☐ napkins

   Serves 10-12.

Preparation: Set out all materials so children can see ingredients. Grease cookie sheets with shortening. Have children wash and dry hands.

Procedure: Preheat oven to 425°. Measure warm water into large mixing bowl. Sprinkle yeast on water and stir until dissolved. Add salt, sugar and flour. Mix and knead dough. Each child rolls small ball of dough into thin rope, then into letter, numeral or other shape. Lay twisted pretzels on greased cookie sheets. Brush pretzels with beaten egg. Bake for 12-15 minutes. Let cool, then brush with small amount of water and sprinkle with salt.

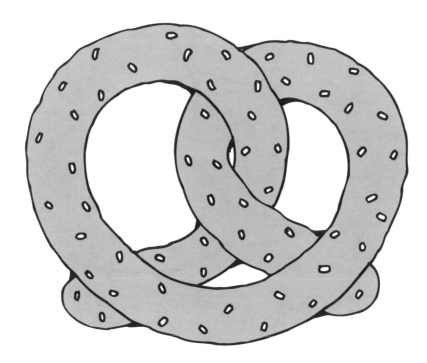

Chow Mein Chewies

Materials Checklist

- ☐ 1 (12-oz.) pkg. butterscotch pieces
- ☐ ½ c. peanut butter
- ☐ 1 (6-oz.) can chow mein noodles
- ☐ 1 c. peanuts
- ☐ measuring cups
- ☐ large saucepan or pot
- ☐ wooden spoon
- ☐ cookie sheet
- ☐ waxed paper
- ☐ spoons
- ☐ napkins

Serves 10-12.

Preparation: Set out all materials so children can see ingredients. Line cookie sheet with waxed paper. Have children wash and dry hands.

Procedure: With adult supervision, children place butterscotch pieces and peanut butter in saucepan. Cook over low heat on stovetop and stir until melted. Remove from heat. Children add noodles and peanuts, then stir well. Children drop spoonfuls of mixture onto waxed paper. Let stand until firm.

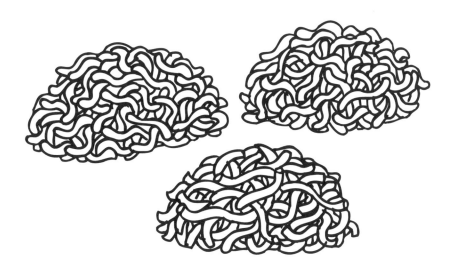

Fresh Fruit with Coconut Dip

Materials Checklist

☐ watermelon, cantaloupe, papaya, mangoes, tangerines, oranges, apples, strawberries, bananas

☐ ½ c. chopped peanuts

☐ 1 small can frozen lemonade (thawed)

☐ 1 c. coconut cream (available in gourmet markets and health food stores)

☐ cutting boards

☐ knives

☐ measuring cup

☐ serving plate

☐ mixing bowl

☐ mixing spoon

☐ small bowls for serving dip

☐ toothpicks

☐ napkins

Serves 12.

Preparation: Set out all materials so children can see ingredients. Have children wash and dry hands.

Procedure: Children peel and cut the fruit into small pieces; then arrange the fruit on serving plate and sprinkle with chopped peanuts. To make the dip, mix the lemonade and coconut cream. Put dip into small bowls. Children use toothpicks to dip fruit into dip.

Burritos

Materials Checklist

- [ ] 1 (2 oz.) pkg. cheddar cheese
- [ ] 1 (8-oz.) can refried beans
- [ ] 6 flour tortillas
- [ ] can opener
- [ ] mixing bowl
- [ ] tablespoon
- [ ] cheese grater
- [ ] microwave oven or electric skillet
- [ ] paper plates
- [ ] napkins

Optional—

- [ ] chopped or sliced olives
- [ ] salsa
- [ ] sour cream
- [ ] chopped onions
- [ ] chopped lettuce

Serves 6.

Preparation: Set out all materials so children can see ingredients. Have children wash and dry hands.

Procedure: In mixing bowl, children take turns grating the cheese. After opening the can of refried beans, children spoon about 3 Tbs. of the refried beans into the center of each tortilla. Sprinkle cheese on top of beans. Fold in each side of tortilla, then fold lower part of tortilla to the center. Fold top of tortilla over lower part to meet at the bottom. Heat the stuffed tortillas in microwave oven or electric skillet. (*Optional:* Children add olives, sour cream, salsa, onions or lettuce after heating tortillas.)

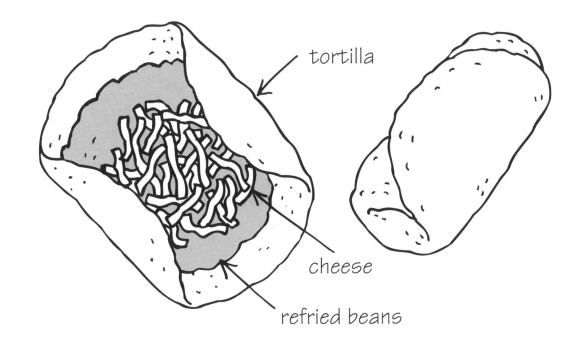

tortilla

cheese

refried beans

Banana and Pineapple Kebobs

Materials Checklist

- ☐ 4 bananas
- ☐ 1 (20-oz.) can pineapple chunks
- ☐ toothpicks or bamboo skewers
- ☐ plastic knives
- ☐ bowl
- ☐ napkins
- ☐ can opener

Serves 8.

Preparation: Drain canned pineapple and place in a bowl. Set out all materials so children can see ingredients. Have children wash and dry hands.

Procedure: Cut bananas into 1-inch (2.5-cm) sections. Children make kebobs, pushing banana and pineapple chunks onto toothpicks or bamboo skewers.

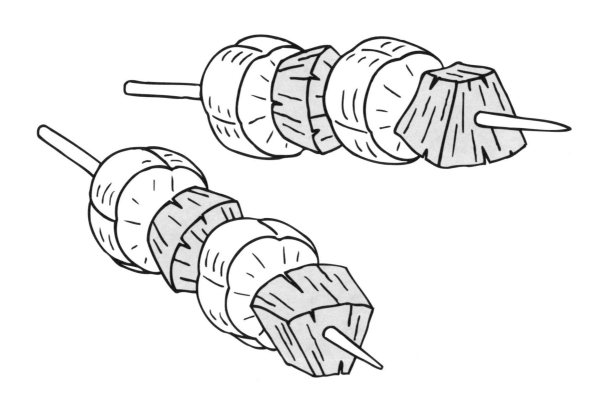

Japanese Pineapple Cream Dessert

Materials Checklist

- ☐ 2 envelopes unflavored gelatin
- ☐ 2 c. water
- ☐ 2 c. milk
- ☐ ¾ c. sugar
- ☐ 1 tsp. almond extract
- ☐ 1 fresh pineapple, cut into cubes
- ☐ measuring cups
- ☐ measuring spoons
- ☐ saucepan
- ☐ wooden spoon
- ☐ 9-inch square cake pan
- ☐ knife
- ☐ paper plates
- ☐ forks

Serves 8-10.

Preparation: Set out all materials so children can see ingredients. Have children wash and dry hands.

Procedure: In a saucepan, sprinkle gelatin over ½ cup hot water; stir until dissolved. Add remaining water, the milk and sugar. Heat, stirring frequently, until mixture is hot, then add almond extract, stirring well. Pour mixture into a 9-inch square cake pan and chill in the freezer to set quickly. Cut dessert into 1-inch (2.5-cm) cubes and serve along with cubes of pineapple. (If making recipe with children, do cooking step early to allow time for dessert to set.)

Russian Two-Cheese Salad

Materials Checklist

☐ 1 (12-oz.) brick white cheese
   (such as Jack or Gouda)

☐ 1 (12-oz.) brick yellow cheese
   (such as mild cheddar)

☐ garlic salt, to taste

☐ 1 bunch green onions

☐ 2 boiled eggs

☐ ½ c. sour cream

☐ 1 loaf brown bread (Russian rye or pumpernickel)

☐ several knives

☐ mixing bowl

☐ wooden spoon

☐ paper plates

☐ cheese graters

☐ cutting boards

☐ measuring cup

   Serves 8-10.

Preparation: Set out all materials so children can see ingredients. Have children wash and dry hands.

Procedure: Children grate the cheeses, chop onions and eggs. Mix cheeses, onions, eggs and sour cream. Each child spreads cheese salad on a slice of bread and may sprinkle garlic salt on top of mixture. (Encourage children to sprinkle garlic salt on just a corner and taste it to see if they like it before sprinkling it on the whole mixture.)

Japanese Bentô Box

Materials Checklist

☐ 4 c. cooked Japanese rice (Be sure to rinse raw rice before cooking so it will be sticky.)

☐ ¼ c. rice vinegar (or white vinegar)

☐ ½ c. sesame oil (or vegetable oil)

☐ 1 Tbs. sugar

☐ carrots

☐ toasted sesame seeds

☐ lettuce

☐ cucumber

☐ Japanese red pickled ginger (available where Asian foods are sold)

☐ small shallow box for each child (such as a candy box)

☐ waxed paper

☐ grater

☐ measuring cups

☐ aluminum foil

☐ green construction paper

☐ scissors

☐ 2 mixing bowls

☐ mixing spoon

☐ vegetable cutting knives

☐ cutting board

☐ a set of chopsticks for each child

Serves 8.

Preparation: Set out all materials so children can see ingredients. Have children wash and dry hands.

Procedure: Children grate carrot, slice cucumber and shred lettuce, then combine vegetables with pickled ginger in a bowl. Children mix vinegar, oil and sugar together in a second bowl, pour it over vegetables and ginger, tossing gently to cover. On a sheet of wax paper, each child shapes ½ cup of rice into two triangles. (If rice is dry, shape with wet hands.) Child sprinkles sesame seeds on the outside edge of the rice triangles.

Each child lines the inside of the bottom of his or her box with foil, pinching to make a wall in the center of the bottom, then pinching foil tightly around the edge of the box. Child places rice triangles in one part of lunch box and adds some of the vegetable mixture in the other part. Child cuts construction paper "sprigs of grass" and places them in the box with the rice triangle. Take Bentô boxes and chopsticks outside for a Japanese-style picnic.

Australian Lamingtons

Materials Checklist

☐ 9×13-inch unfrosted yellow cake, cut into 2-inch (5-cm) cubes

☐ 3 c. powdered sugar

☐ ⅓ c. cocoa

☐ 3 Tbs. butter or margarine, melted

☐ ½ c. boiling water

☐ 3 c. shredded coconut

☐ measuring cups

☐ measuring spoons

☐ saucepan

☐ bowl

☐ pie tin

☐ mixing spoon

☐ forks

☐ knife

☐ wire rack

☐ paper plates

Serves 12-15.

Preparation: Set out all materials so children can see ingredients. Have children wash and dry hands.

Procedure: Mix sugar and cocoa in a bowl, then add boiling water and melted butter. Mix well until smooth. Set icing bowl in a saucepan about one-fourth full of simmering water to keep it warm. Place coconut in a pie tin next to the saucepan and a wire rack on the other side of the coconut, in assembly-line fashion. Using forks, dip each square of cake into the hot icing and let the excess icing drip off. Then roll iced cake in coconut on all sides and place on wire rack to cool.

coconut

hot water

wire rack

International Games • **Primary**
Follow the Leader
(Universal Game)

Procedure: Select one child to be the leader. Players line up single file behind the leader, arms-length apart. Leader then walks in any manner and in any direction, while the rest of the players follow behind, imitating his or her actions. Leader tries to fool his or her followers by surprising them with different actions (such as a somersault, duck waddle, jumping jack, etc.). Change leaders every few minutes.

Lame Chicken (Chinese Relay Game)

Materials Checklist

☐ 20 sticks about 2 feet (.6 m) long

☐ chalk or tape

Preparation: Place 10 sticks on the ground, parallel to each other and about 1 foot (.3 m) apart (see sketch). Use chalk or tape to make a starting line about 15 feet (4.5 m) from the first stick. Make an identical course using other 10 sticks.

Procedure: Divide group into two even teams.

Teams stand in single file lines behind starting lines. At teacher's signal, first player on each team hops up to the sticks and hops over each stick to pick up the last one. Player then hops back over each stick, places stick about 1 foot (.3 m) in front of the first stick, and hops back to tag next player in line. The next player repeats the process. First team to have all players complete the course wins. (Note: Players may hop on one foot or two.)

15'

1'

sticks

International Games • **Primary**
Red Light, Green Light
(American Game)

<u>Materials Checklist</u>

☐ chalk or tape

☐ measuring stick

Preparation: Use chalk or tape to make a starting line and a finish line, at least 15 feet (4.5 m) apart.

Procedure: Choose one player to be "It." "It" stands behind the finish line. Players stand behind starting line. Game begins when "It" turns his or her back to the players and calls, "Green light!" Players then run towards the finish line. When "It" calls, "Red light," players must stop running and freeze in position. "It" turns around to face the runners and tries to catch someone moving. "It" may send anyone caught moving back to the starting line. Game continues until one runner is close enough to tag "It." The player that tags "It" becomes the new "It." (The closer the runners get to the finish line, the quicker the intervals between "green light" and "red light.")

Starting line

Red light!

Finish line   ← "It"

15'

Le Furet (Belgian Game)

Materials Checklist

☐ small ball

Procedure: Choose one player to be the "Searcher." Remaining players line up against a wall, sitting down with their hands behind their backs, elbow-to-elbow. The Searcher stands with back to wall, six steps away from players.

Play begins when the Searcher tosses the ball (Le Furet) toward the wall so that one of the players can catch it. The players then secretly pass the ball back and forth, behind their backs, while the Searcher tries to find the ball. If the ball reaches either end of the line, it may be thrown out over the Searcher's head and the Searcher has to start over again. However, if the Searcher finds the ball before it reaches the end of the line, the player who is holding it becomes the new Searcher.

Presohan (Filipino Tag)

Materials Checklist

☐ chalk or masking tape

☐ measuring stick

For each player—

☐ empty soda can

Preparation: Use chalk or tape to make a small *X* on the ground. Mark a "safety line" about 8 feet (2.4 m) from the *X* as shown in sketch.

Procedure: Choose one player to be the "Prisoner." Prisoner sets his or her can on the *X* and stands behind it. Give each player a soda can. Players stand behind the "safety line." Players take turns throwing their cans at the Prisoner's can. When a player hits the Prisoner's can, he or she must try to retrieve own can without being tagged by the Prisoner. The Prisoner may not tag a player until he or she (the Prisoner) has returned own can to the *X.* When a player is tagged, he or she becomes the new Prisoner. If a player does not hit the Prisoner's can, he or she must wait until another player has hit the can. As soon as another player has hit the Prisoner's can, all players who have missed the can may run and try to retrieve their cans without being tagged.

Forceball
(British or Australian Ball Game)

Materials Checklist

☐ one basketball or kick ball

☐ chalk or masking tape

☐ measuring stick

Preparation: Use chalk or tape to make two parallel lines about 3 yards (2.7 m) apart.

Procedure: Divide group into two teams. Players line up side by side with legs apart and feet touching as shown in sketch. Teams face each other. The object of the game is to roll the ball between the legs of the players on the opposing team. Players bat the ball to the opposite team using only their hands. Players cannot move their feet. Teams get one point every time the ball rolls through the opposing team's legs. Team with the most points wins the game.

Egyptian Stick Race

<u>Materials Checklist</u>

☐ measuring stick

For each player—

☐ one 4-foot (1.2-m) stick

Procedure: Players stand in a large circle about 8 feet (2.4 m) apart from each other. Each player faces the middle of the circle and holds a stick upright, in the left hand, with one end on the ground. At teacher's signal, each player lets go of his or her own stick and races to catch the stick of the player to the right, before it touches the ground. If the stick touches the ground, the player who failed to catch it is out, along with the stick. (Play a practice round first, until children feel confident.) Circle shrinks in size as more and more players are out. Last player remaining in the game is the winner.

Jumper Bean (American Game)

Materials Checklist

☐ tube sock

☐ stuffing (such as rags or beans)

☐ yarn or string

☐ rope or heavy cord

☐ scissors

☐ chalk or masking tape

☐ measuring stick

Preparation: Fill foot of the sock with stuffing. Secure stuffing inside sock by tying a piece of yarn or string around the opening. Cut rope or cord into a 5-foot (1.5-m) length. Tie rope or cord around one end of the sock (sketch a). Use chalk or tape to make a large circle at least 10 feet (3 m) in diameter (sketch b).

Procedure: Choose one person to be "It." "It" stands in the center of the circle. Players stand around "It" while remaining in the circle. "It" holds the end of the rope and slowly swings the sock around the circle near the ground. Players try to jump over the sock to avoid getting hit. When a player gets hit by the sock, he or she is out of the game and leaves the circle. A player is also out of the game if he or she steps outside of the circle. If "It" hits any player above the knees, he or she is out and the person who was hit becomes the new "It." Game continues until only one player is left inside the circle. Last player left inside the circle becomes the new "It." (For a larger group, make rope longer and circle bigger.)

Gorelki (Russian Line Tag)

Materials Checklist

☐ rope or masking tape

☐ measuring stick

Procedure: Choose one player to be "It." Divide group into two teams. Teams line up in pairs as shown in sketch. Mark a line about 10 feet (3 m) from the front of the line. "It" stands behind line. When "It" says, "Last pair run," the last pair runs up the outside of their lines and join hands at the front of the lines before "It" can tag either one of them. If "It" tags a player, tagged player becomes the new "It" and they switch places.

Tlachtli (Mexican Ball Game)

Materials Checklist

☐ light, rubber ball

☐ chalk or rope

☐ markers to distinguish one team from another (such as a handkerchief or cloth strip tied to the arm)

☐ measuring stick

☐ coin

Preparation: Use chalk or rope to mark a 15×40-yard (13×36-m) rectangular playing area. Mark lines to divide the playing area into four even sections—two end courts and two middle courts (see sketch).

Procedure: Divide group into two teams of 5-10 players. Distribute markers to distinguish one team from another. Choose one player from each team to be the team captain. Have team captains call a coin flip to see which team is first. Teams take sides, facing each other, as in soccer. Players are assigned to stay in an end court or middle court.

Play begins when teacher tosses ball into the air at center line. Each team tries to bump the ball to the other team's end line. The ball can be hit only with the hips, shoulders, knees or back—no hands, feet or heads. If the ball ends up on the ground so that players have no way to hit it, teacher tosses it up again. When a team scores a goal, the team gets 5 points and play starts over in the center. First team to score 25 points wins.

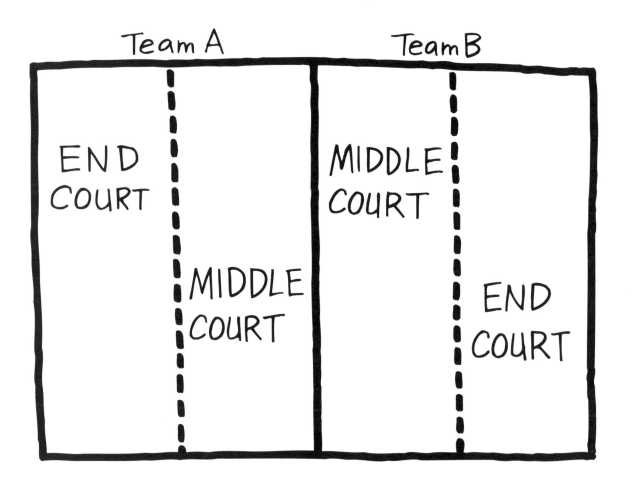

Farm/ Country

Theme craft ideas can be found in the
Country Crafts for Kids book,
available from Gospel Light.

Farm/Country Decorations

Start with a scarecrow and bales of hay placed around the room. Cover tables with gingham or calico cloths. Baskets of fruit and vegetables and jars of jam or honey make great centerpiece items. A few rag rugs, pitch forks, rocking chairs, straw hats, a banjo and a harmonica will help to create atmosphere. Play country music on a cassette player and have the host or hostess dress in overalls, a gingham shirt and a straw hat or a calico dress with a sunbonnet.

Use the clip art in this book to create the following farm or country party items:

- Barnyard animal name tags

- Invitations
- Programs
- Hoe-down song sheets

Also, use the clip art to create the following life-sized wall decorations:

- Field of crops with a tractor
- Barn and barnyard with animals
- Country porch
- Fruit trees
- Vegetable garden

Farm/Country Clip Art

The Big Book of Theme Parties, Snacks and Games © 1997 by Gospel Light. Permission to photocopy granted.

39

Strawberry Country Dip

Materials Checklist

- ☐ 1 (8 oz.) pkg. softened cream cheese
- ☐ 1 small pkg. strawberry flavor JELL-O
- ☐ ¼ c. milk
- ☐ 1 (8 oz.) container of non-dairy dessert topping (such as Cool Whip)
- ☐ fruit for dipping (strawberries, apples, bananas, grapes)
- ☐ mixing bowl
- ☐ measuring cups
- ☐ wire whisk or mixer
- ☐ knives
- ☐ cutting board
- ☐ serving spoon
- ☐ small bowls
- ☐ toothpicks
- ☐ paper plates

Makes 1½ c. of dip.

Serves 6-8.

Preparation: Set out all materials so children can see ingredients. Have children wash and dry hands.

Procedure: Have several children cut up fruit and place in bowls while others make the dip. Children making the dip place cream cheese into a mixing bowl. Next they add JELL-O and milk. Children beat mixture with wire whisk or mixer until well blended and smooth. Blend in whipped topping. Spoon dip into small bowls. Children use toothpicks to lower fruit into dip and enjoy!

Homemade Butter and Biscuits

Materials Checklist

- ☐ measuring cups
- ☐ teaspoons
- ☐ large mixing bowl
- ☐ mixing spoon
- ☐ shortening
- ☐ baking sheet
- ☐ knives for spreading
- ☐ paper plates

For butter—

- ☐ 1 pt. whipping cream
- ☐ salt
- ☐ plastic qt. jar with lid

For biscuits—

- ☐ 2 c. biscuit mix
- ☐ ½ c. milk

   Makes 12 small biscuits and approximately 1 cup of butter.

Preparation: Set out all materials so children can see ingredients. Lightly grease baking sheet with shortening. Have children wash and dry hands.

Procedure: Have children measure out the biscuit mix and milk into large bowl. They take turns stirring the mixture until it is a lumpy dough. Next, let children drop teaspoonfuls of dough onto baking sheet. Bake the biscuits at 400° for 10 minutes or until golden brown. While the biscuits are baking, have children place pint of whipping cream into plastic quart jar, with your assistance. Children take turns shaking the jar until cream thickens, in about 15 minutes. Pour off excess liquid, mash to make butter and form into a ball. Sprinkle with salt to taste and blend with a spoon. Use butter as a spread on fresh homemade biscuits.

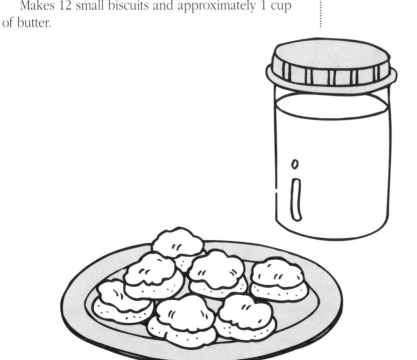

Animal Cutout Sandwiches

Materials Checklist

- ☐ 1 (large) loaf of soft bread
- ☐ 1 small tub of softened butter
- ☐ 1 (16-oz.) pkg. processed cheese slices
- ☐ large animal-shaped cookie cutters
- ☐ butter knives
- ☐ napkins

    Serves 10-12.

Preparation: Prepare a sample Animal Cutout Sandwich in advance for demonstration. Set out materials so children can see ingredients. Have children wash and dry hands.

Procedure: Children butter two slices of bread, then place cheese slice between bread slices. Use cookie cutter to cut animal shape out of sandwich.

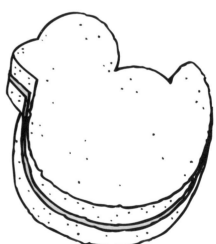

Farm/Country Snacks

Dirt Cups

Materials Checklist

- ☐ 2 c. cold milk
- ☐ 1 large pkg. instant chocolate pudding
- ☐ 3½ c. thawed nondairy dessert topping (such as Cool Whip)
- ☐ 1 (1-lb.) pkg. chocolate sandwich cookies
- ☐ measuring cups
- ☐ rolling pin
- ☐ large resealable plastic bags
- ☐ mixing bowl
- ☐ mixing spoon
- ☐ 9-oz. clear plastic cups
- ☐ spoons

Optional—

- ☐ Gummy Worms and Frogs to decorate tops of dirt cups

Makes 10 (6-oz.) servings.

Preparation: Set out all materials so children can see ingredients. Have children wash and dry hands.

Procedure: Children mix pudding and milk together according to package directions. Let stand five minutes. Next, children place cookies into plastic bags and seal. (Make sure all of the air is out of the bags.) Children use rolling pin to crush cookies. Children gently stir whipped topping and half of the crushed cookies into pudding, until mixture is all one color. Children place one spoonful of remaining crushed cookies into bottom of each plastic cup. Fill cups about three-fourths full with pudding mixture. Top each cup with a small amount of the crushed cookies and serve. (*Optional:* Tear Gummy Worms in half and insert into "dirt.")

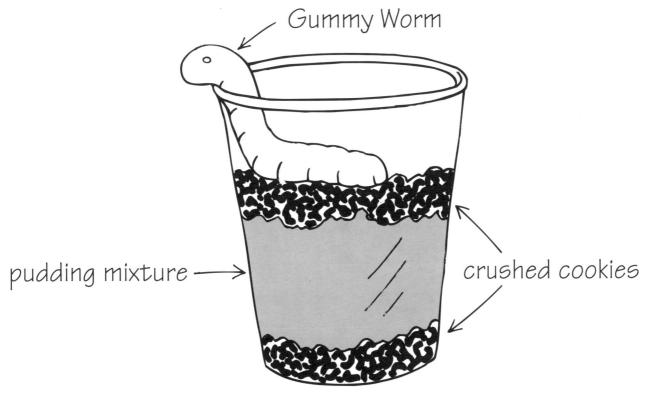

Gummy Worm

pudding mixture

crushed cookies

Garden Rounds

Materials Checklist

- ☐ carrots
- ☐ cucumbers
- ☐ celery
- ☐ zucchini
- ☐ 1 (8-oz.) pkg. cream cheese
- ☐ 1 (18-oz.) jar of peanut butter
- ☐ paper plates
- ☐ knives
- ☐ cutting board
- ☐ vegetable peeler
- ☐ paper plates

    Serves 12-16.

Preparation: Set out all materials so children can see ingredients. Have children wash and dry hands.

Procedure: Help children peel and then slice carrots, cucumbers and zucchini into round shapes. Cut celery into small lengths. Let children make "sandwiches" with vegetables, cream cheese and/or peanut butter. Serve on paper plates.

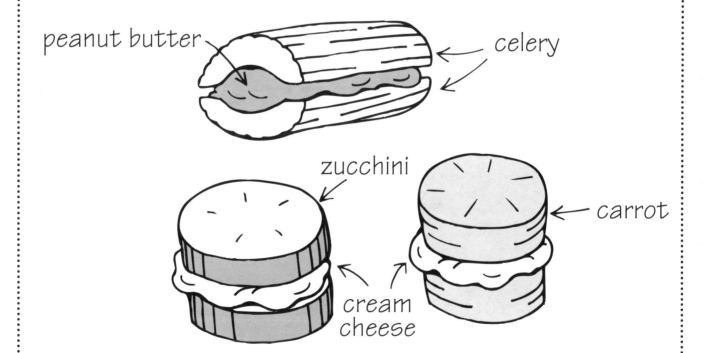

Farmer's Energy Rolls

Materials Checklist

☐ 1 c. raisins

☐ 1 c. finely chopped dates

☐ 4 Tbs. honey

☐ 2 pkgs. graham crackers (or more as needed)

☐ large mixing bowl

☐ mixing spoon

☐ large plastic resealable bags

☐ rolling pin

☐ measuring cups

☐ measuring spoons

☐ napkins

Makes 15-20 small balls.

Preparation: Set out all materials so children can see ingredients. Have children wash and dry hands.

Procedure: Let children use rolling pin to crush graham crackers in plastic bags. Make sure air is out of bags before rolling begins. Children place raisins, dates and honey into mixing bowl, then mix in crushed graham crackers until mixture is moist. Form into small balls and enjoy.

Homemade Ice Cream

Materials Checklist

- ☐ 1 qt. half-and-half cream
- ☐ ¾ c. sugar
- ☐ ⅛ tsp. salt
- ☐ 1½ tsp. vanilla extract
- ☐ large mixing bowl
- ☐ mixing spoon
- ☐ 2 (1-lb.) coffee cans with lids
- ☐ 2 (3-lb.) coffee cans with lids
- ☐ cracked ice
- ☐ rock salt
- ☐ measuring cups
- ☐ measuring spoons
- ☐ bowls
- ☐ spoons

Optional—

- ☐ fresh fruit such as bananas, strawberries, peaches
- ☐ crushed cookies

Serves 6-8.

Preparation: Set out all materials so children can see ingredients. Have children wash and dry hands.

Procedure: Combine cream, sugar, salt and vanilla in mixing bowl. Stir until sugar and salt are completely dissolved. Pour the mixture into both 1-lb. coffee cans, dividing mixture evenly. Put the lids on the cans, then place inside the 3-lb. coffee cans. Pack larger can alternating cracked ice with rock salt, then put lids on cans. Let children roll cans around on the ground until ice cream is firm, approximately 15-20 minutes. During this process, take lid off and stir every five minutes. When hardened, store ice cream in freezer until ready to serve.

(*Optional:* Freeze ice cream mixture in an old-fashioned crank ice cream freezer. Add fresh fruit and crushed cookies to make flavored ice cream.)

Apple Trees

Materials Checklist

☐ 8 small apples

☐ 1 (10-oz.) pkg. stick pretzels

☐ 1 (1-lb.) block of cheese

☐ round toothpicks or other instruments for poking holes (ice pick, cuticle sticks, clean nails, shish kebob skewers)

☐ cutting board

☐ knives

☐ napkins

Serves 8.

Preparation: Prepare an Apple Tree sample in advance for demonstration. Set out all materials so children can see ingredients. Have children wash and dry hands.

Procedure: Have children cut cheese block into small cubes. Next, using a toothpick or other instrument, they poke holes in their apples. Children push pretzel sticks into cheese cubes, then put pretzel sticks into holes in apple. They will have a garden full of "apple trees"—their very own orchard! (*Note:* Serve immediately. Pretzels become soggy where inserted in apples.)

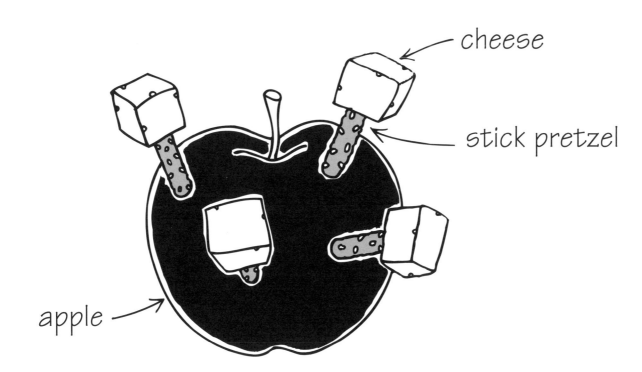

cheese

stick pretzel

apple

String-Along Relay

Materials Checklist

☐ ball of twine for each team (length of twine must be the same in each ball)

Procedure: Divide group into two or more teams. Teams line up single file. When a signal is given, teams begin to unroll a ball of twine over their heads.

Each team continues to unwind the ball of twine up and down the line until it is completely unrolled. The first team to use up the entire ball of twine wins.

Variation: Alternate passing the ball of twine over the head and through the legs until entire ball of twine is unrolled.

Team A

Team B

The Big Drip

Materials Checklist

☐ 2 buckets

☐ water

☐ 2 large sponges

☐ 2 empty 2-liter soda bottles

☐ measuring stick

☐ chalk or rope

Preparation: Fill buckets with water. Use chalk or rope to make starting line. Place buckets at starting line 6 feet (1.8 m) apart. Place soda bottles approximately 12-15 feet (3.6-4.5 m) away from water buckets (see sketch).

Procedure: Divide group into two teams. Each team lines up behind its bucket. Give the first player in each line a sponge and instruct them to dip sponges in water, run to bottle, squeeze water into bottle, run back and give sponge to the next person in line, then go to the end of the line. Continue in relay fashion until bottle is full of water (or until water level reaches a designated mark).

Shoes in a Muddle

Procedure: Children remove their shoes and socks and put them in a pile in the center of play area. Children then line up across the yard, shoulder-to-shoulder, facing pile. At a given signal, children run to pile, find their own shoes and socks, put them on and run back to starting line. First person back wins.

Variation: If some of the children are not wearing socks, have them form an additional team. The two teams do not compete against each other, but the children within each team compete with their own teammates.

The Earthworm

Procedure: Choose a player to be the "Earthworm." At a signal the Earthworm begins chasing other players. Each player tagged by the Earthworm must hold hands to form an Earthworm line. Only the outside hands of the Earthworm line can be used for tagging. The Earthworm chases other untagged players until all have been caught. The last person caught becomes the new Earthworm.

Farmer's Harvest

Materials Checklist

☐ three soft rubber or sponge balls

☐ measuring stick

Procedure: Divide group into four teams. Give each team the name of a fruit or vegetable. Teams line up in a square so that there is one team standing on each of the four sides at least 20 yards (18 m) apart. Choose one person from one team to be the "Farmer." Give Farmer the balls. Farmer stands in the middle of the square and calls out the names of two of the fruits or vegetables (e.g., "Corn!" "Apples!"). All the corn and all the apples run to exchange places. The Farmer tries to "pick" one or more of the fruits/vegetables by throwing ball at him or her. The first three fruits or vegetables "picked" then become the new Farmers. (Farmers who have picked fruit sit out until a new game begins.) Play continues until all fruits/vegetables have been picked.

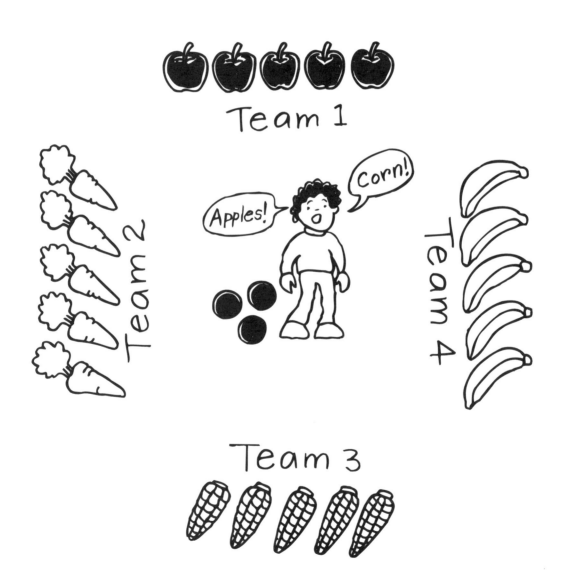

Corn Huskers' Race

Materials Checklist

☐ measuring stick

For each team—

☐ a large paper bag

For each player—

☐ an unshucked ear of corn

Optional—

☐ large pot

☐ water

Procedure: Place bags approximately 6 feet (1.8 m) apart. Divide group into equal teams. Teams line up 12-15 feet (3.2-4.5 m) from bags. Give each player an ear of corn. Team members take turns running to bag, shucking ear of corn and running back to team. First team with all corn shucked is the winner. (*Optional:* Wash and boil corn and serve for snack.)

Variation: Have a few volunteers take off shoes and attempt to shuck corn using only bare feet.

Barnyard Bluff

☐ handkerchief or scarf

Procedure: Designate boundaries of the playing area. Choose one person to be "It" and cover his or her eyes with the handkerchief. Have each player choose a barnyard animal. Players will make their animal sounds during the game. The object of the game is for "It" to chase the other players, trying to locate them by sound. When "It" manages to tag someone, the player tagged must in turn be blindfolded and is the new "It." Players change animal sounds before each new game begins.

Scarecrow Relay

Materials Checklist

☐ three or four large boxes

☐ measuring stick

For each box—

☐ a straw hat

☐ pair of work gloves

☐ pair of large boots

☐ shirt

Procedure: Divide class into three or four teams. Each team lines up about 15 feet (4.5 m) from their box. The first player of each team runs to the team's box, puts on one item of clothing, runs back to team, takes off the clothing item and hands it to the next person in line. The second person puts on the item of clothing, runs to the box, puts on another item of clothing, runs back to team, takes off items and hands them to next person. Continue procedure until all items are being worn. (Or until everyone has a chance to run in the relay.)

Drip the Well Dry

Materials Checklist

☐ 2 buckets

☐ water

☐ 2 large sponges

☐ 2 empty 2-liter soda bottles

☐ masking tape

☐ measuring stick

Preparation: Fill buckets with water. Place buckets at starting line 6 feet (1.8 m) apart. Place masking tape around each soda bottle at matching designated marks. Place soda bottles approximately 12-15 feet (3.6-4.5 m) away from water buckets (see sketch).

Procedure: Divide group into two teams. Each team lines up arms-length apart between bucket and soda bottle, facing the bucket. First player in each line dips a sponge into water, and passes sponge over his or her head to the next player. Next player, in turn, passes the sponge underneath his or her legs to the next player. Over-head and under-legs sequence continues until sponge reaches player closest to the bottle. Last player then squeezes remaining water from sponge into bottle and runs to the head of the line to repeat process. First team to fill bottle to designated mark wins. (Note: Children will get wet playing this game!)

Farm/Country Games •Junior

Grape Smash Bash

Materials Checklist
☐ several large bunches of grapes (preferably red grapes)
☐ 1 large plastic garbage bag
☐ scissors
☐ bucket of water or garden hose
☐ measuring stick

Optional—
☐ pebbles or marbles

Procedure: Cut garbage bag to make two plastic mats. Place mats 6 feet (1.8 m) apart. Divide group into two equal teams. Teams line up 20 feet (6 m) from mats. All players take off shoes and socks, and roll up pants. Give each player two grapes. First player on each team places grapes between his or her toes. At teacher's signal, players run to plastic mats with grapes between toes. Players then drop grapes on mats and run back to team to tag next player. When last player returns to his or her line, all team members run to plastic mat and stomp and smash grapes. First team to smash all their grapes is the winner. Use bucket of water or hose to wash players' feet. (Note: If you prefer, pebbles or marbles may be substituted for grapes. Delete stomping.)

Swing Your Partner

Procedure: Designate boundaries of the playing area. Choose one player to be "It" and one player to be "Chaser." Remaining players choose partners, hook elbows and form a circle with Chaser and "It" inside the circle. The object of the game is for Chaser to try and tag "It." At any time, "It" may hook elbows and swing any other player. As soon as "It" hooks elbows with another player, he or she becomes the new partner, and is "safe," while the old partner immediately becomes the new "It" and unlocks elbows to be chased. When Chaser manages to tag "It," the player tagged becomes the new Chaser. Partners may swing in place, while the Chaser is chasing "It."

Bible Times

Theme craft ideas can be found in the
Bible Times Crafts for Kids book, available from Gospel Light.

Bible Times Decorations

Use decorated butcher paper to make your door look like a gate in a wall to a Bible Times city (see illustration below). Place low tables and pillows or rugs in the room. Create a marketplace with booths to sell fabric, pottery and baskets of foods. Include a life-sized Bible Times marketplace scene on the wall. Play Middle Eastern music on a cassette player. Burn some sandalwood or other incense in dishes on the tables or in a tent made of sheets, rope and stakes. The host or hostess dresses in Bible Times costume.

Use the clip art in this book to create the following

Bible Times party items:
- Bible character name tags (with the guest's name and a Bible Times name for the party)
- Bible Times scroll invitations
- Scroll programs

Also, use the clip art in this book to create the following life-sized Bible Times wall decorations:
- Camels, sheep, goats, doves
- Marketplace
- Bible Times homes
- Desert scene with tents

63

Matzoh Bread

Materials Checklist

- [ ] 8 hardboiled eggs
- [ ] salt
- [ ] water
- [ ] saucepan
- [ ] small glass bowl
- [ ] 2 c. whole wheat flour and flour for dusting hands
- [ ] glass mixing bowl
- [ ] mixing spoons
- [ ] measuring cups
- [ ] oil
- [ ] fork
- [ ] baking sheet
- [ ] rolling pin
- [ ] paper plates
- [ ] waxed paper

   Serves 8.

Preparation: Hard boil eggs. Set out all materials so children can see ingredients. Grease baking sheet with oil. Have children wash and dry hands.

Procedure: Demonstrate the mixing of Matzoh bread with child volunteers. Mix 2 cups wheat flour with ½ to ¾ cup water to form dough. Dust lightly with flour. Children flour hands and knead dough for 3-5 minutes. Divide into 6-8 balls. Children press balls flat with hands, then roll with rolling pin to ⅛-inch (.3-cm) thickness. Place on baking sheet. Prick with fork. Sprinkle with salt. Bake 8-10 minutes in 450° oven. Matzohs can be eaten while soft or left in oven once it has been turned off to become crisp.

Children mix salt with water in glass bowl, then peel and eat eggs dipped in salt water along with the Matzoh bread.

Conversation: **The Hebrews had a traditional meal called Passover. God gave instructions as to what Passover foods were to be eaten and why. Today let's prepare two special Passover foods (Matzoh bread and hard-boiled eggs).**

salt

water

eggs

Bible Times Snacks

Raisin Cake

Materials Checklist

- ☐ 4 eggs
- ☐ ½ c. honey
- ☐ ½ c. whole wheat flour or whole wheat cake flour
- ☐ ½ tsp. salt
- ☐ 2½ c. raisins
- ☐ 1 c. slivered almonds
- ☐ shortening
- ☐ measuring cups
- ☐ measuring spoons
- ☐ electric mixer or egg beater
- ☐ mixing bowls
- ☐ mixing spoons
- ☐ 9-inch (22.5-cm) square baking pan
- ☐ paper plates
- ☐ napkins

Serves 16.

Preparation: Set out all materials so children can see ingredients. Grease baking pan with shortening. Have children wash and dry hands.

Procedure: Direct child volunteer to beat eggs in large bowl until fluffy. Allow other children to measure and beat in honey, flour, salt, raisins and almonds. Pour batter into greased pan. Bake 30-40 minutes in 350° oven. Cake will be the consistency of fruit cake.

Conversation: **In Bible Times, honey cakes were a common dessert. Today we will bake a honey cake using raisins. Raisins and honey were used to sweeten foods because sugar was not available.**

raisins

eggs

almonds

Sweet Millet Balls

Materials Checklist

- [ ] saucepan with lid
- [ ] water
- [ ] 1½ c. chopped dried fruit such as figs, dates, apricots or raisins
- [ ] 1 c. cooked millet
- [ ] ½ c. each chopped almonds, walnuts and pistachio nuts
- [ ] measuring cups
- [ ] mixing bowl
- [ ] mixing spoon
- [ ] baking sheet
- [ ] napkins

Makes 2 dozen balls.

Preparation: Precook millet by boiling for 20 minutes, covered. Let stand for seeds to open. Set out all materials so children can see ingredients. Have children wash and dry hands.

Procedure: Direct volunteers to mix chopped fruit, millet, walnuts and pistachios in bowl. Allow children to shape the mixture into 1½-inch (3.75-cm) balls. Roll balls in chopped almonds, place on baking sheet and refrigerate before serving.

Conversation: **Today we will be making a snack using dried fruits, nuts and millet. Millet is a cereal that is very high in fiber. The children in Bible Times enjoyed making a special dessert like the snack we are making.**

cooked millet

chopped fruit

Haroseth

Materials Checklist

- ☐ 2 medium apples
- ☐ ½ c. chopped nuts
- ☐ ½-¾ c. grape juice
- ☐ ½ tsp. cinnamon
- ☐ ½ c. raisins
- ☐ cutting board
- ☐ measuring cups
- ☐ measuring spoons
- ☐ mixing bowl
- ☐ mixing spoons
- ☐ small paper cups
- ☐ plastic spoons
- ☐ knives

Serves 6-8.

Preparation: Set out all materials so children can see all ingredients. Have children wash and dry hands.

Procedure: Direct child volunteers to core and chop apples into small pieces. Place apples into mixing bowl. Children add nuts, grape juice, cinnamon and raisins to bowl and mix all ingredients together. Serve immediately in small cups.

Conversation: **Haroseth is a mixture of chopped fruits and nuts. It was an important symbolic food eaten at Passover. It reminded the Jews of their hard work in Egypt and of the mortar, or special "cement," used to build the Egyptian monuments. Jesus and His disciples probably ate Haroseth at the Last Supper, the night before He died.**

raisins

chopped nuts

Cinnamon Yogurt

Materials Checklist

- [ ] ½ pound cream cheese or vanilla yogurt
- [ ] 1 tsp. ground cinnamon
- [ ] 1-1½ tsp. honey
- [ ] mixing bowl
- [ ] mixing spoon
- [ ] measuring spoon
- [ ] melba toast or stoned wheat crackers
- [ ] knives
- [ ] paper plates

  Serves 6-8.

Preparation: Set out all materials so children can see ingredients. Have children wash and dry hands. Set out cream cheese at room temperature to soften.

Procedure: Direct volunteers to mix cream cheese or yogurt with cinnamon and honey in bowl until smooth. Children spread on toast or crackers and serve on paper plates.

Conversation: **Today we will prepare a special food served at celebrations in Bible Times. In Bible Times, goat cheese was a common food to eat. It was soft and creamy, like our cream cheese or yogurt. Sugar was not available in Bible Times, so honey was used to sweeten their foods.**

Barley Cakes

Materials Checklist

- ☐ 1½ c. warmed milk
- ☐ ½ tsp. salt
- ☐ 3 Tbs. honey
- ☐ 3½ c. barley flour
- ☐ measuring cups
- ☐ measuring spoons
- ☐ mixing bowl
- ☐ mixing spoons
- ☐ baking sheet
- ☐ paper plates
- ☐ napkins

Optional—

- ☐ ¾ c. raisins

Makes 3 dozen small cakes.

Preparation: Set out all materials so children can see ingredients. Have children wash and dry hands.

Procedure: Children take turns measuring, adding and mixing the milk, salt, honey, barley flour and raisins (if desired) in mixing bowl. Next, have children shape the dough into small balls. (Dough will be sticky.) Place the balls on the baking sheet and flatten them slightly with the heel of your hand. Bake the Barley Cakes at 400° for about 20 minutes.

Conversation: **In Bible Times, shepherds had to stay out in the fields watching their sheep. They couldn't go home for lunch. So they took Barley Cakes to eat. Barley Cakes lasted for several days and were a healthy meal.**

Fruit/Nut Mix

Materials Checklist

- [ ] ½ c. each dried pitted prunes, apricots, pears and banana chips
- [ ] ½ c. each unsalted peanuts, cashews, almonds and walnuts
- [ ] ground cinnamon
- [ ] ground cloves
- [ ] measuring cups
- [ ] large mixing bowl
- [ ] mixing spoon
- [ ] small paper cups or bowls

  Serves 8.

Preparation: Set out all materials so children can see ingredients. Have children wash and dry hands.

Procedure: Children take turns measuring and adding ingredients to large mixing bowl and add cinnamon and cloves to taste. Stir or toss until mixture is evenly mixed. Serve in small cups or bowls.

Conversation: **God filled the Garden of Eden with plants that provided food for Adam and Eve to eat. Adam and Eve could pick from the nut and fruit trees in the garden to prepare a snack very much like the one we will prepare today.**

Pita Bread

Materials Checklist

☐ whole wheat pita bread halves

☐ 1 (8-oz.) pkg. softened cream cheese

☐ 1 (6-oz.) can pitted black olives

☐ knives

☐ cutting board

☐ paper plates

Serves 12.

Preparation: Set out all materials so children can see ingredients. Have children wash and dry hands.

Procedure: Direct children to cut Pita Bread halves into halves again to make triangles. Children spread cream cheese inside the pita triangles. Children chop olives and sprinkle them on cream cheese. Have plenty on hand because children enjoy this Bible Times snack!

Conversation: **In Bible Times, wheat flour was used only when baking for special guests and special occasions. A woman would serve flat wheat bread with goat's cheese to the guests she had in her home. Let's spread cream cheese, similar to soft goat's cheese, in our Pita Bread to enjoy a Bible Times snack.**

cream cheese

pita bread

chopped olives

Gingered Watermelon

Materials Checklist

- ☐ watermelon half
- ☐ 1 c. water
- ☐ ½ c. white grape juice
- ☐ 1 Tbs. honey
- ☐ 1 piece grated candied ginger
- ☐ measuring cups
- ☐ measuring spoon
- ☐ saucepan
- ☐ melon ballers
- ☐ large bowl
- ☐ paper cups
- ☐ spoons

Serves 8-10.

Preparation: Set out all materials so children can see ingredients. Have children wash and dry hands.

Procedure: Direct some of the children to use melon ballers to make bite-size pieces of watermelon and place in large bowl. Oversee the remainder of the children in combining the water, grape juice and honey in the saucepan. Heat gently; add ginger. After the mixture has cooled, pour it over the melon and refrigerate before serving. Spoon melon into paper cups.

Conversation: **Today we will prepare a snack similar to what the Israelites ate in Egypt. Watermelon grew easily near the Nile River, but the ginger was a rare, expensive spice brought to Egypt from faraway countries.**

water

Grape Juice

GINGER

Honey

Barley Stew with Lentils

Materials Checklist

- ☐ ⅓ c. chopped onion
- ☐ ½ c. chopped celery
- ☐ ½ c. chopped carrots
- ☐ ½ pound beet greens or spinach
- ☐ 5 Tbs. butter
- ☐ 6 c. water or stock
- ☐ 1 c. dried lentils
- ☐ ½ c. barley
- ☐ ⅛ tsp. rosemary
- ☐ 2 tsp. salt
- ☐ 2 tsp. ground cumin
- ☐ large soup pot
- ☐ large spoon
- ☐ measuring cups
- ☐ measuring spoons
- ☐ cutting board
- ☐ knives
- ☐ bowls
- ☐ spoons
- ☐ napkins

Serves 12-15.

Preparation: Set out all materials so children can see ingredients. Have children wash and dry hands. Precook barley and lentils before class.

Procedure: Direct child volunteers in chopping and measuring the onion, celery, greens and carrots. In large soup pot, sauté the onion, celery and carrots in the butter. Add the water or stock, lentils, barley, rosemary, salt, and cumin. Bring to a boil, turn down heat, and cook until vegetables are tender. Add greens for the last 15 minutes of cooking. Serve in bowls.

Conversation: **The first Christians didn't eat meat every day like many of us do. They got protein from eating lots of grains and beans. Today we will make a stew using barley (a grain) and lentils (a bean). Many New Testament Christians probably ate stew like this.**

Scroll Relay

Materials Checklist

☐ butcher paper

☐ masking tape or rope

☐ measuring stick

Preparation: Use paper to make two scrolls for each team. Use tape or rope to mark two starting lines on each playing area, about 20 feet (6 m) apart.

Procedure: Divide group into two teams. Each team then divides into two equal lines and two halves of team stand opposite each other behind starting lines (see sketch). Give a scroll to the first player in each line on one side. At a given signal the players with the scrolls run toward the other half of their team. When teammates meet, they exchange scrolls, run around each other and return to their own half of the team. The scroll is given to the next player in line who repeats process. After running, players go to the end of their lines. Play continues until the first players are back in the starting place with the scrolls.

Team 1

20 ft.

Team 2

Noah's Cloudburst

Procedure: Have children join hands in a circle and pretend to form a cloud. Circle stretches out as far as possible, then goes inward, then stretches out again until the circle breaks. Repeat as time and interest allow. If time permits, children may form small clouds of three or four players.

Walk Across the Desert

Materials Checklist

☐ felt pen

For each player—

☐ 1 index card

  Preparation: Using felt pen, draw a different kind of line on each index card (see sketch).

  Procedure: Children sit in a row along one side of the playing area. Place an index card facedown in front of each player. When teacher calls out, "Walk across the desert!" children turn their cards over and walk across the playing area in the manner suggested by the lines on the cards. When children have completed their "walks," collect cards, shuffle them and pass them out again. Play until each child has had a chance to try out several cards.

 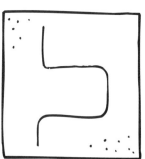  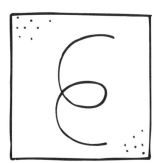

Roman Ball Toss

Materials Checklist

☐ 2 or more small balls

Procedure: Group stands in a large circle, with players standing several feet apart. Choose one volunteer to pick up any dropped balls and hand them back to first player. Play begins when any one player tosses a ball to the person next to him or her. That player tosses the ball to the next person. Play continues with each player quickly tossing the ball to the next person. If the ball is dropped, volunteer returns it to the first player. As the first ball is going around the circle, put another ball into play. Keep adding balls until they are all in play. The game is over when all the balls have gone around the circle a set number of times. In ancient times, slaves stood outside the circle to pick up any dropped balls. Balls were made of leather or cloth.

Gather on the Mountain

Materials Checklist

☐ chalk or masking tape

Preparation: Using chalk or masking tape, make triangles (large enough for most children on one team to stand inside; one triangle for each team) on the floor or ground.

Procedure: Divide group into two or more equal teams and see how many children each team can get on its "mountain" (inside the triangle). Anything is legal, as long as no part of the body is touching the floor outside the triangle. Set a time limit and have team competition.

Tug-of-War

Materials Checklist

☐ 20 feet (6 m) of thick, smooth rope

☐ chalk or masking tape

☐ measuring stick

Note: A rope which is too thin or too rough may "burn" the hands of those pulling.

Preparation: Using chalk or tape, mark a dividing line on playing area.

Procedure: Explain to children that drawings from ancient times show children playing tug-of-war. Divide group into two equal teams. Teams form two lines, holding on to the rope on opposite sides of the dividing line. Leave a space of about 6 feet (1.8 m) between the two teams. The object is to be the first team to pull the other team over the dividing line.

Carpenter's Race

Materials Checklist

For each team—

☐ hammer

☐ nail

☐ piece of thick scrap wood

Preparation: For each team, start a nail into the piece of wood just until it stays firmly in place.

Procedure: Divide group into teams. Each team forms a circle and sits on the floor or ground. Distribute a hammer and a piece of wood with nail to the first player on each team. At a given signal, players use the hammer to hit the nail once and pass hammer and wood to the player on their left. Procedure is repeated until one team has successfully driven the nail all the way into the wood.

Variation: Game can also be played relay fashion. Teams form lines and hammers and wood are placed on the ground at a distance from teams. Each player races across playing area, hits the nail once with the hammer and runs back across playing area, tags the next person and goes to the end of the line. Play continues until one team has successfully driven the nail into the wood.

Team A

Team B

Scroll Dodge

Materials Checklist

☐ old towel

☐ masking tape or string

Preparation: Fold towel so it's 12-18 inches (30-45 cm) long. Roll up the folded towel and tape or tie to hold it in a roll. If you have a large group, prepare two or three towels.

Procedure: Children stand around the edges of playing area with "scroll" on the floor or ground in the center of the area. At a given signal, players try to grab the towel and throw it at others while avoiding being hit themselves. The player who has the towel may take only two steps, but all others may run around as much as they please. If a player is hit with the towel, he or she must stand on the sidelines. Play continues until there is only one player remaining.

Optional: Start the game with several towels and reduce the number of towels as the number of active players is diminished.

Coats-of-Many-Colors

Materials Checklist

☐ colored newspaper comics

☐ staplers

☐ staples

Procedure: Divide group into pairs. Give each pair a stapler, staples and comics. Tell the players that they must fashion coats that include sleeves, a back and front. At a given signal, pairs begin to fashion coats by stapling comics together. Game ends when one pair has completed coats for both players and put them on. (At the end of game, allow additional time for all players to complete coats.)

Follow the Cloud

Materials Checklist

☐ rope or chalk

☐ measuring stick

For each player—

☐ 1 white balloon

Preparation: Using rope or chalk, mark a goal line at one end of the playing area.

Procedure: Divide group into teams. Teams line up one behind the other approximately 15 feet (4.5 m) from the goal line. At a signal, the first player on each team blows up his or her balloon and lets it go toward the goal line. Player must then go where it lands, stop, and blow it up again and let it go. This procedure is repeated until balloon crosses the goal line. The player then picks up the balloon, runs back and tags the next player on the team, who repeats procedure. Game ends when all players on one team have made it to the goal line and back again.

15'

Mountain/Camping

Theme craft ideas can be found in the **Mountain Crafts for Kids** book,
available from Gospel Light.

Mountain/Camping Decorations

Re-create a mountain camping trip with a few simple decorations. Use potted pine trees, pine branches, pine cones and potpourri or a candle with pine scent. Then put up a tent and place sleeping bags, hiking boots and jackets inside. Set up a camp table and benches. Inflate a river raft to set out with oars. Use stones and logs to build a pretend campfire. A camping lantern, compass, wildlife book, flashlight, packets of trail mix and canteen help complete the scene. Play a cassette containing the sounds of running water, birds, frogs and crickets on a cassette player. Come dressed in jeans, boots, outdoors jacket or vest and cap.

Use the clip art in this book to create the following mountain party items:
- Mountain wildlife name tags
- Camping invitations
- Programs
- Wildlife guide

Also, use the clip art in this book to create the following life-sized mountain wall decorations:
- Deer, bears, mountain goats and eagles
- River rafters
- Mountain climbers
- Mountain scene with a lake

Mountain/Camping Clip Art

The Big Book of Theme Parties, Snacks and Games © 1997 by Gospel Light. Permission to photocopy granted.

Mountain Energy Bars

Materials Checklist

- ☐ 1 box graham-cracker crust mix
- ☐ ½ c. shredded coconut
- ☐ 1 (18-oz.) pkg. chocolate or carob chips
- ☐ 1 (18-oz.) pkg. butterscotch chips
- ☐ ½ c. chopped nuts
- ☐ 1 (14-oz.) can sweetened condensed milk
- ☐ measuring cups
- ☐ mixing bowl
- ☐ mixing spoon
- ☐ 9×13-inch baking pan
- ☐ knife
- ☐ napkins

Serves 24.

Preparation: Line a baking pan with graham-cracker crust mix. Set out all materials so children can see ingredients. Have children wash and dry hands.

Procedure: Place shredded coconut, chocolate or carob chips, butterscotch chips and chopped nuts in mixing bowl. Mix well and then spread over crust. Pour can of sweetened condensed milk over top and bake at 350° for 30 minutes. Cool and cut into bars.

The Big Book of Theme Parties, Snacks and Games © 1997 by Gospel Light. Permission to photocopy granted.

Tasty Trail Balls

Materials Checklist

- ☐ 2¼ c. peanut butter
- ☐ 6½ c. powdered milk
- ☐ 1 c. brown sugar
- ☐ 1 to 2 c. granola
- ☐ large mixing bowl
- ☐ measuring cups
- ☐ paper plates
- ☐ napkins

   Serves 15-20.

Preparation: Set out all materials so children can see ingredients. Have children wash and dry hands.

Procedure: Children measure peanut butter, powdered milk, brown sugar and granola into a large bowl. Then children take turns mixing ingredients with their hands. Then they form 1-inch balls by rolling mixture between their hands.

Nutty Fruit Rounds

Materials Checklist

- ☐ 2 c. dried fruit (raisins, dates, apricots)
- ☐ 2 c. nuts (walnuts, pecans, almonds)
- ☐ meat grinder or food processor
- ☐ mixing bowl
- ☐ mixing spoon
- ☐ paper plates

Serves 10-12.

Preparation: Set out all materials so children can see ingredients. Have children wash and dry hands.

Procedure: Place dried fruits and nuts in a meat grinder or food processor and mix well. Scoop out mixture and place in mixing bowl. Give each child some of the mixture which can then be formed into 1-inch (2.5-cm) to 1½-inch (3.75-cm) balls.

Chicken Spread

Materials Checklist

- ☐ 1 (5-oz.) can chicken, drained
- ☐ 1 (8-oz.) pkg. softened cream cheese
- ☐ 1 (8.5 oz.) box rye snack crackers
- ☐ mixing bowl
- ☐ mixing spoon
- ☐ plastic knives
- ☐ paper plates
- ☐ napkins

    Serves 8-10.

Preparation: Set out all materials so children can see ingredients. Drain chicken. Allow cream cheese to soften. Have children wash and dry hands.

Procedure: Place chicken and softened cream cheese in mixing bowl and stir together. Children then spread mixture on top of rye snack crackers. (Tuna may be substituted for the chicken.)

crackers

Campout Cocoa

Materials Checklist

For each child—

- ☐ 1 pkg. instant hot cocoa mix
- ☐ boiling water
- ☐ miniature marshmallows
- ☐ Styrofoam cup
- ☐ plastic spoon

Serves 1.

Preparation: Set out all materials so children can see ingredients. Boil water.

Procedure: Pour envelope of instant hot cocoa mix into cup. Add water, leaving 1-inch space from top of cup. Stir with spoon to mix thoroughly. Float marshmallows on top of hot cocoa.

Trail Crumbs

Materials Checklist

- ☐ 2 c. peanuts, chopped
- ☐ ½ c. dates, chopped
- ☐ ½ c. shredded coconut
- ☐ 1 c. sunflower seeds
- ☐ ½ c. carob chips
- ☐ mixing bowl
- ☐ mixing spoon
- ☐ measuring cups
- ☐ 8 small paper cups or plastic sandwich bags

  Serves 8.

Preparation: Set out all materials so children can see ingredients. Have children wash and dry hands.

Procedure: Place chopped peanuts, chopped dates, shredded coconut, sunflower seeds and carob chips in mixing bowl. Stir together and serve to children in small paper cups or plastic sandwich bags.

Hikers' Salad

Materials Checklist

- ☐ 1 (8-oz.) bottle Italian salad dressing
- ☐ 1 container alfalfa sprouts
- ☐ toothpicks
- ☐ paper plates

For each child—

- ☐ 1 slice of ham
- ☐ 1 slice of cheese
- ☐ 1 lettuce leaf

  Serves 1.

Preparation: Prepare a Hikers' Salad sample in advance for demonstration. Set out all materials so children can see ingredients. Wash vegetables. Have children wash and dry hands.

Procedure: Place a slice of ham and slice of cheese on top of a lettuce leaf. Sprinkle with some Italian salad dressing. Add a handful of alfalfa sprouts and roll up the lettuce leaf. Secure with a toothpick and serve on a paper plate.

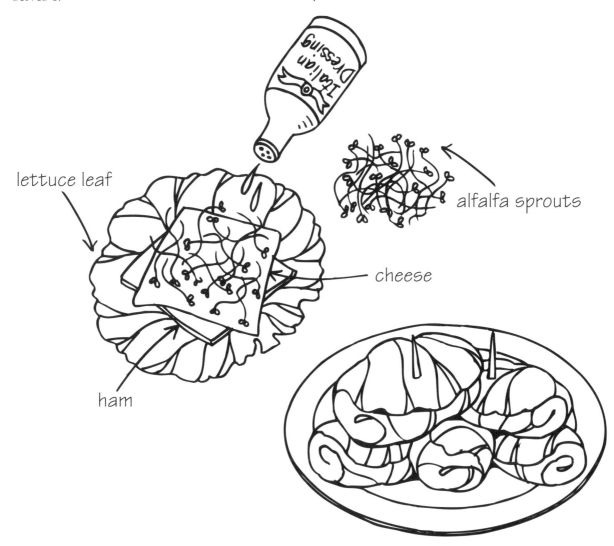

lettuce leaf

alfalfa sprouts

cheese

ham

Fruit Leather

Materials Checklist

- ☐ 5 c. of fresh fruit such as berries, peaches, plums, apricots
- ☐ shortening
- ☐ measuring cups
- ☐ knives
- ☐ cutting board
- ☐ blender
- ☐ saucepan
- ☐ cookie sheet
- ☐ plastic spatula
- ☐ napkins

Optional—

- ☐ grape-nuts® cereal

Preparation: Set out all materials so children can see ingredients. Wash fruit thoroughly, then peel and slice fruit. Grease cookie sheet with shortening. Have children wash and dry hands.

Procedure: Place fruit in a blender and mix well. Pour mixture into saucepan and heat through. Pour mixture back into blender and blend a second time. Pour contents onto cookie sheet and spread with a plastic spatula. Bake at 150° for eight hours. Let cool and tear into strips before serving. For an added treat, sprinkle top of fruit leather with grape-nuts® cereal before baking.

Trail's-End Fruit Punch

Materials Checklist

- ☐ 1 (2 ltr.) bottle ginger ale or club soda
- ☐ 1 Tbs. orange juice concentrate
- ☐ 1 c. water
- ☐ 1 tsp. lemon juice
- ☐ pitcher
- ☐ mixing spoon
- ☐ measuring cups
- ☐ measuring spoons
- ☐ ice
- ☐ small cups

Makes 12 (4-oz.) drinks.

Preparation: Set out all materials so children can see ingredients. Have children wash and dry hands.

Procedure: Pour ginger ale, orange juice concentrate, water and lemon juice into pitcher. Stir ingredients together. Serve over ice in small cups.

River Raft

Materials Checklist

- ☐ 1 pkg. large pretzel sticks (about ½ inch in diameter)
- ☐ small jar of peanut butter
- ☐ large rectangular crackers such as Norwegian flat bread or Matzoh
- ☐ knives
- ☐ napkins

Serves 8-10.

Preparation: Set out all materials so children can see ingredients. Have children wash and dry hands.

Procedure: Give each child a paper napkin, one rectangular cracker, 10 pretzel sticks, a knife and access to the peanut butter. To form raft, children spread peanut butter on crackers and place pretzel sticks "raft fashion" on peanut butter.

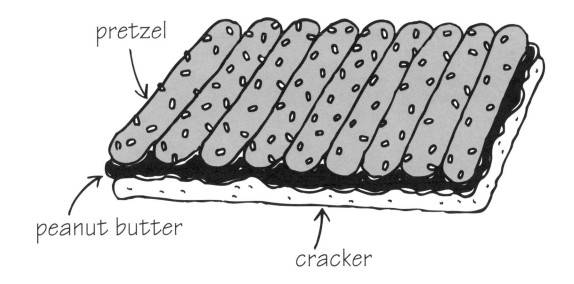

pretzel

peanut butter

cracker

Grizzly Bear Paws

Materials Checklist

- ☐ 2 cans (10 count) extra large refrigerator biscuits
- ☐ 80 whole blanched almonds
- ☐ ¼ tsp. cinnamon
- ☐ ⅓ c. honey
- ☐ 1 c. softened butter
- ☐ baking sheets
- ☐ scissors
- ☐ foil
- ☐ permanent felt pen
- ☐ small bowl
- ☐ measuring cups
- ☐ measuring spoons
- ☐ wooden spoon
- ☐ bread knives

Serves 20.

Preparation: Tear or cut foil into 8-inch (20-cm) lengths—one for each child. Set out all materials so children can see ingredients. Preheat oven to 400°. Have children wash and dry hands.

Procedure: Give each child a foil piece, an uncooked biscuit and a bread knife. Child uses felt pen to letter name on foil. Child places biscuit on foil and stretches it slightly into an oval, then cuts three slits for toes (see sketch). Insert the rounded end of an almond into the end of each toe. The pointed end will look like a claw. Almonds must be pushed halfway into dough or they will pop out during baking. Place biscuits (on foil pieces) on ungreased baking sheets about 2 inches (5 cm) apart, spreading toes. Bake biscuits for 12 minutes or until they are golden brown. While biscuits are baking, children take turns measuring and stirring together the butter, honey and cinnamon. When biscuits are done, serve with honey butter.

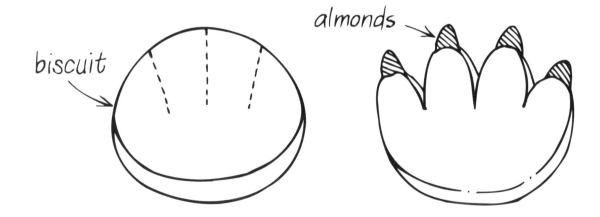

biscuit

almonds

Fallen Logs

Materials Checklist

- ☐ 1 large loaf sliced wheat bread
- ☐ 1 (28-oz.) jar peanut butter
- ☐ raisins
- ☐ plastic knives
- ☐ paper plates

Serves 20.

Preparation: Set out all materials so children can see ingredients. Have children wash and dry hands.

Procedure: Give each child a paper plate, a plastic knife and a slice of bread. Children spread peanut butter on bread. Then children place some raisins on the peanut butter and roll the bread into a "log."

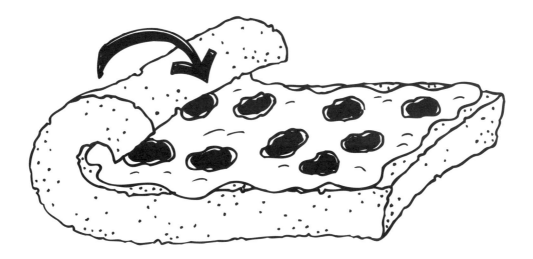

Mountain Masterpiece

Materials Checklist

☐ felt pen

☐ masking tape

For each team—

☐ large sheet of paper

☐ box of crayons

Optional—

☐ newspaper

Preparation: Tape sheets of paper to wall or table. (You may want to tape newspaper on the wall around each paper to protect the wall from crayon marks.) In the corner of each paper, letter a list of instructions for drawing a simple mountain scene. Each paper should have the same instructions. Make the instructions complex enough so each team member will have at least one item to draw (see sketch).

Procedure: Divide group into teams of no more than four players. Give each team a box of crayons. To help beginning readers, read instruction list aloud with children. The first player on each team races to the paper, reads the first instruction, draws the item and checks off what he or she has drawn. First player then runs back to team, tags second player who races to paper, reads second instruction and continues picture. Allow time for each team to successfully complete its masterpiece.

Draw 1. an eagle
2. perched in a green tree
3. high in the mountains
4. overlooking a blue lake

or

Draw 1. a hiker
2. wearing a red backpack
3. carrying a fishing pole
4. crossing a stream

Canoe Races

Materials Checklist

- ☐ 4 large sheets of cardboard
- ☐ craft knife
- ☐ heavy-duty stapler and staples or strapping tape
- ☐ broad felt marker
- ☐ rope or masking tape
- ☐ measuring stick

Preparation: Draw a canoe shape on each sheet of cardboard (see sketch). Cut out canoe shapes. Staple ends together to make two canoes which are open at the bottom. Use rope or masking tape to make starting line. Make goal line about 20-30 feet (6-9 m) away from starting line by also using rope or masking tape. Place canoes at starting line.

Procedure: Divide group into two teams. Each team lines up behind their canoe. At a given signal, two or three players climb into their canoe, hold onto the sides, race to the finish line, turn and race back to the starting line. Players climb out of canoe and next two or three players climb in and repeat process.

Hiker Hugs

Procedure: Choose one player to be "It." The remainder of group spreads out and runs around the play area. "It" calls out a number between two and six. As soon as the number is called, children run and form a group hug with that number of people. (E.g., If "three" is called, groups of three children hug together.) Of those left out from each hug, choose one player to be the new "It."

Three!

Eagles and Owls

Materials Checklist

☐ ropes or masking tape

☐ measuring stick

Procedure: Using ropes or masking tape, designate two goal lines 30-40 feet (9-12 m) apart on opposite sides of playing area. Divide group into two teams—the Eagles and Owls. Teams line up facing each other four or five feet apart. Leader shouts out the name of one team. If leader yells, "Eagles," the Eagles must turn around and run toward their goal line, with the Owls chasing them. If any of the Owls succeed in tagging a member of the Eagles before he or she crosses the line, player is considered a captive of the Owls and must aid the Owls when play continues. Game ends when one team captures all the members of the opposite team.

Thirsty Hiker Relay

Materials Checklist

☐ 4 buckets

☐ water

For each player—

☐ tin camping cup

Optional—

☐ timer

Procedure: Divide group into two teams. Each team lines up single file with a bucket of water on one end and an empty bucket on the other. Each team member has a tin camping cup. The object of the game is to transfer the water from one bucket to the other by pouring the water from cup to cup down the line. Game is over when one team has transferred all of the water to the empty bucket.

Variation: Use a timer and play for a given amount of time to see which team can transfer the most water from bucket to bucket.

The Big Book of Theme Parties, Snacks and Games © 1997 by Gospel Light. Permission to photocopy granted.

End-of-Trail Tag

Materials Checklist

☐ 1 bandana

Procedure: Choose one person to be "It." Have the rest of the group form a circle holding hands. Place the bandana in the back pocket of one of the players.

"It" runs around the outside of the circle trying to grab the bandana while the circle quickly rotates one direction, then the opposite direction, trying to save the bandana from being caught. If the bandana is caught, "It" joins the circle and a new "It" is chosen.

bandana

Summit Shoe-Scramble

<u>Materials Checklist</u>

For each player—

☐ 1 blindfold (bandana)

Procedure: Have players sit in a circle, take off their shoes and toss them in the middle. Mix up the shoes. Blindfold each player, then mix up the shoes again. On the word "go," have children scramble to the shoe pile and try to determine which shoes are theirs by trying on different shoes. When players think they've found their own shoes, have them put on both shoes. Play continues until everyone is wearing a pair of shoes. Remove blindfolds to see who has matching shoes and who doesn't.

Leapin' Logs

Materials Checklist

☐ large, grassy playing area

Procedure: Divide group into two teams. An extra player can be the caller. Teams sit facing each other (see sketch). Players on each team extend their legs, keeping knees together and having soles of feet touching to form pairs with players from the opposite team. Leave enough space between pairs of legs ("logs") for players to hop over. Pairs count off down the line. Then the caller shouts a number and the pair whose number has been called jumps up, steps over the legs of the others, races around the outside, then over the remaining legs and returns to original place. The first player back in place wins a point for his or her team. The game is over when every pair has had a turn to race.

Sunrise, Sunset

Procedure: Group sits cross-legged in a close circle with backs toward center of circle and arms linked. When teacher calls out, "Sunrise, Sunset," the circle must stand up, circle to left one complete revolution and sit down without unlinking arms.

Variation: If group is large enough, divide into teams and have teams race to successfully complete revolution in a given amount of time.

Lake Ness Creature

Materials Checklist

☐ Nerf ball

☐ 2 ropes

☐ large playing area

Procedure: Define two rope lines on opposite ends of the playground. The lines are the "shores" and the "lake" is the area in between. One player is selected to be the creature. All other players are fishes. The object of the game is for the creature to tag the fishes with the ball before they can run safely to the opposite shore. The creature wanders around the lake while the fishes gather behind one of the shore lines. Then the creature calls out, "Fishes, fishes, swim in my lake!" At this command, the fishes must swim (run) across the lake to the opposite shore. If one is tagged or hit by the ball, he or she is frozen in place. All tagged fishes remain stationary and become the creature's "arms" in the next round. When the creature again invites the fishes to swim in the lake, they can be tagged by the outstretched arms of the stationary fishes, as well as by the roaming creature. Play until there is one fish remaining, who then becomes the new creature.

shore

lake

shore

Mountaineer Hobble

Materials Checklist

☐ a few pebbles

☐ rope or masking tape

☐ measuring stick

Procedure: Using rope or masking tape, designate a goal about 20 feet (6 m) away. Have players remove their shoes and socks. Divide group into equal teams. Each team forms a single line. Give the first player of each team a pebble to put between his or her toes. On the word "go," have each player hobble to the goal and back without losing control of the pebble. If the pebble is dropped, player must pick it up with his or her toes and continue the race. Then he or she tags the next player in line and gives him or her the pebble. Game continues until all players on a team have had a turn.

20 feet

Pioneer/Western

Theme craft ideas can be found in the **Pioneer Crafts for Kids** book, available from Gospel Light.

Pioneer/Western Decorations

Bring your guests back to the Old West pioneer days by using a few simple decorations. Place bales of hay around the room and scatter sawdust on the floor. Place cowboy or pioneer hats and boots, banjos, harmonicas, quilts, barrels, lanterns, saddles and other horse gear around the room. Play country-western music on a cassette player. Use old wooden tables and chairs and/or tablecloths of gingham or calico. Host or hostess dresses in cowboy or pioneer costume.

Use the clip art in this book to create the following items:
- Cowboy or pioneer name tags
- Old West invitations
- Programs

Also, use the clip art in this book to create the following life-sized wall decorations:
- Horse, buffalo, oxen
- Covered wagon
- Log cabin

Pioneer/Western Clip Art

Frontier Biscuits

Materials Checklist

☐ 2 c. sifted all-purpose flour

☐ 3 tsp. baking powder

☐ 1 tsp. salt

☐ ⅓ c. shortening

☐ 1 c. milk

☐ mixing bowl

☐ sifter

☐ measuring cups

☐ measuring spoons

☐ fork

☐ tablespoons

☐ pastry blender or 2 knives

☐ napkins

☐ cookie sheet

Makes 20.

Preparation: Set out all materials so children can see ingredients. Have children wash and dry hands.

Procedure: Preheat oven to 450°. Sift flour with baking powder and salt into medium bowl. Cut shortening into flour mixture with a pastry blender or two knives (used scissors fashion), until mixture resembles coarse cornmeal. Make a well in the center. Pour in 1 cup milk all at once. Stir quickly around the bowl, with a fork. Drop dough, by tablespoonfuls, onto lightly greased cookie sheet. Bake for 10 minutes or until golden-brown.

Prairie Cobbler

<u>Materials Checklist</u>

☐ 1 (1-lb. 13-oz.) can of sliced peaches

☐ can opener

☐ small paper cups

☐ 1 c. plain yogurt

☐ 1 c. granola

☐ cinnamon

☐ measuring utensils

☐ spoons

☐ napkins

　Serves 8.

Preparation: Set out all materials so children can see ingredients. Have children wash and dry hands.

Procedure: Place sliced peaches into small paper cups. Children top their peaches with 1 Tbs. plain yogurt, 1 Tbs. granola and a dash of cinnamon.

Thirst-Quenchin' Cider

Materials Checklist

☐ 1 (32-oz.) can apple juice

☐ 1 (16-oz.) bottle of club soda

☐ mixing spoon

☐ pitcher

☐ paper cups

Serves 8.

Preparation: Set out all materials so children can see ingredients. Have children wash and dry hands.

Procedure: Mix together apple juice and club soda. Pour into paper cups and serve.

Sunflower Dip

Materials Checklist

- [ ] 1 c. processed cheese spread
- [ ] ½ c. sunflower seeds
- [ ] 1 Tbs. wheat germ
- [ ] raw vegetable sticks such as carrots, celery, etc.
- [ ] mixing bowl
- [ ] mixing spoon
- [ ] measuring spoons
- [ ] measuring cups
- [ ] paper plates

Serves 10-12.

Preparation: Set out all materials so children can see ingredients. Have children wash and dry hands.

Procedure: Mix together processed cheese spread, sunflower seeds and wheat germ. Serve with raw vegetable sticks.

Chuck Wagon Chili

Materials Checklist

☐ 1 (40-oz.) can of chili or homemade chili, if desired

☐ 1 (1-lb.) block of cheese

☐ saucepan or large pot

☐ small Styrofoam cups

☐ cheese grater

☐ spoons

☐ napkins

☐ serving spoon

Serves 10.

Preparation: Set out all materials so children can see ingredients. Heat chili in saucepan or large pot. Have children wash and dry hands.

Procedure: Children take turns shredding cheese with cheese grater. Spoon canned or homemade chili into small Styrofoam cups. Top with cheese.

cheese

Johnny Cakes

Materials Checklist

- ☐ 1 small container of maple syrup
- ☐ 1 small jar of honey or molasses
- ☐ corn bread or corn muffin mix
- ☐ measuring cup
- ☐ water
- ☐ mixing bowl and spoon
- ☐ square baking pan or muffin tin
- ☐ knives
- ☐ paper plates
- ☐ napkins

    Serves 8-12.

Preparation: Prepare corn bread or muffins according to directions on package. Cut corn bread into squares. Set out all materials. Have children wash and dry hands.

Procedure: Spread maple syrup, honey or molasses on top of warm corn bread squares or muffins.

Wagon Wheel Snackwich

Materials Checklist

- [ ] 1 (16-oz.) jar processed cheese
- [ ] 6 English muffins
- [ ] 1 pkg. sliced bologna
- [ ] 1 small can sliced black olives
- [ ] knives
- [ ] can opener

Serves 12.

Preparation: Set out all materials so children can see all ingredients. Have children wash and dry hands.

Procedure: Cut English muffins in half. Children cut bologna into thin strips. Then they spread processed cheese on English muffin halves. Children place one olive slice in the center of English muffin and arrange bologna strips around center like the spokes of a wagon wheel. Broil until warm.

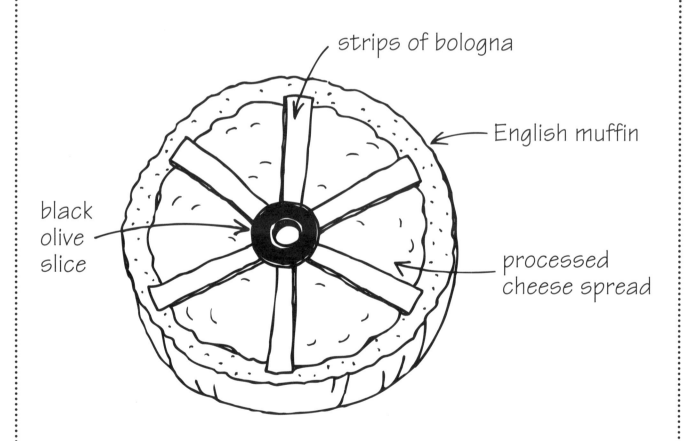

strips of bologna

English muffin

black olive slice

processed cheese spread

Spotted Pup

Materials Checklist

- ☐ 1½ c. uncooked long-grain rice
- ☐ ⅓ c. brown sugar
- ☐ 4 c. milk
- ☐ ½ c. raisins
- ☐ measuring cups
- ☐ large saucepan with lid
- ☐ small Styrofoam cups
- ☐ mixing spoon
- ☐ spoons

Serves 6-8.

Preparation: Set out all materials so children can see ingredients. Have children wash and dry hands.

Procedure: Combine rice, brown sugar, milk and raisins in saucepan. Simmer, uncovered, for about 45 minutes or until milk is absorbed, stirring occasionally. Cover, remove from heat and let stand for 15 minutes. Serve Spotted Pup warm, in Styrofoam cups.

Aunt Addie's Applesauce Pie

Materials Checklist

- ☐ 1 (12-oz.) can buttermilk biscuits
- ☐ 1 (23-oz.) jar chunky applesauce
- ☐ brown sugar
- ☐ cinnamon
- ☐ baking sheet
- ☐ knives
- ☐ spoons
- ☐ paper plates

  Serves 10.

Preparation: Set out all materials so children can see ingredients. Bake biscuits according to directions on can. Slice biscuits in half. Have children wash and dry hands.

Procedure: Heat applesauce in microwave oven or saucepan. Place a spoonful of warm, chunky applesauce on bottom half of biscuit. Sprinkle with brown sugar and cinnamon. Replace biscuit top to make a small "pie."

Sarsaparilla Floats

Materials Checklist

- [ ] 1 (2-ltr.) bottle of root beer
- [ ] ½ gal. vanilla ice cream
- [ ] 8 (8-oz.) mason canning jars or other glass jars
- [ ] ice cream scoop
- [ ] drinking straws
- [ ] plastic spoons

Serves 8.

Preparation: Set out all materials so children can see ingredients. Have children wash and dry hands.

Procedure: Place one scoop of vanilla ice cream into mason jar. Pour root beer into mason jar to fill. Serve with drinking straw and spoon. Explain that sarsaparilla was a popular pioneer drink. It was very similar to root beer and was made from roots and barks mixed with molasses.

Animal Guessing Game

Procedure: Choose one child to be "It" and one child to be the "Chooser." The child who is "It" must stand with his or her face to the wall, with eyes closed. Players then begin moving around the room or yard. The Chooser whispers the name of an animal to a child, who then imitates the noise of that animal.

"It" tries to guess the name of the animal and the name of the child making the noise. If "It" guesses correctly, he or she changes places with the Chooser. If "It" guesses incorrectly, he or she changes places with the child who made the animal sound.

Pioneer Pass Around

Materials Checklist

☐ cassette of children's music

☐ cassette player

☐ any pioneer-type object that children can easily pass around circle

For each player—

☐ 1 chair

Preparation: Place chairs in a circle.

Procedure: Children sit in chairs. As music is played, children pass pioneer object around circle. When music stops, the child holding the object must stand for the remainder of game. Start music, and have children continue passing object. Whenever the object is passed to a player who is standing, he or she must lift up one foot and pass object under his or her leg before passing it to the next person. If a child who is already standing is caught with the object a third time, he or she must pass object under his or her leg and turn around once, then pass object on. Game continues until all players are standing.

Wagon Team Pull

Materials Checklist

☐ rope or masking tape

Preparation: On playing area, make a line using the rope or tape.

Procedure: Divide group into two "wagon" teams and name a "wagon master" for each team. On opposite sides of the line, team members line up behind wagon master and take hold of each other around the waist. Wagon masters grasp wrists, across the line. The object of the game is to pull the opposite team over the line. The game is not over until an entire wagon team has been pulled over the line.

Blind-Man's Bluff

Materials Checklist

☐ handkerchief or scarf

Procedure: Designate the boundaries of the playing area. Choose one player to be "It" and cover his or her eyes with the handkerchief. The object of the game is for "It" to chase the other players, trying to locate them by the sound of their footsteps or other noises made as they try to avoid being caught. When "It" manages to tag someone, the player tagged must in turn be blindfolded and is the new "It."

"It"

Drop the Handkerchief

Materials Checklist

☐ handkerchief

Procedure: Group forms one large circle. Choose one player to be "It." "It" walks around the circle and drops the handkerchief at the feet of another player. The player must then chase "It" around the perimeter of the circle and try to tag "It" before he or she arrives at the space where the chase began. If "It" is not tagged, the two players switch places and the new "It" continues the game in a similar fashion. If "It" is tagged, he or she remains "It" for another turn.

"It"

Graces

Materials Checklist
☐ measuring stick

For each pair of players—
☐ 4 12-inch (30-cm) dowels
☐ 1 medium-sized wooden embroidery hoop

Procedure: Divide group into pairs. Each pair stands approximately 10 feet (3 m) apart and faces each other. Each player holds two dowels crossed at the ends and places the hoop on the crossed ends. The hoop is thrown by quickly uncrossing the dowels in an upward motion. The partners throw their hoop back and forth.

Cross the Creek

<u>Materials Checklist</u>

☐ 2 lengths of rope or masking tape

☐ measuring stick

Preparation: Make a line on the ground for the "starting point." Make a second line, called the "creek," 10 yards (9 m) from the first line.

Procedure: Players line up at the starting point and in succession run to the creek. Once at the creek, players first hop on one foot, then take a long step, then a long jump. Those who cover the greatest distance in one hop, skip and jump are the winners.

starting point

10 yards

creek

Crazy Coach Ride

Procedure: Group sits in a circle. Assign every two or three children to represent a necessary part of the coach—seats, wheels, windows, etc. One player stands in the middle of the circle and calls for any part of the coach. The children representing that part must jump up and exchange places with each other while the caller tries to take an empty spot. The player left standing without a spot then becomes the caller in the middle. Every now and then the caller may call for the entire coach and all players must rise and change places. The caller runs to an empty spot and the person left without a place to sit becomes the caller.

Hog Call

Materials Checklist

☐ large grassy playing area

Optional—

☐ blindfolds

Procedure: Divide the group into pairs. Each pair chooses a pair of items by which to be called. (For example: Hearts and Flowers; Beans and Franks; Bow and Arrow; etc.) Each partner then chooses one of the items. (For example: Becky is "Bow" and Aaron is "Arrow.") Players scatter around the playing area, close their eyes and start shouting their partner's item. (*Optional:* Blindfold all the players.) The object of the game is for partners to find each other using only the sound of their voices. Game ends when all pairs are reunited and the last players open their eyes.

Safari

Theme craft ideas can be found in the
Safari Crafts for Kids book,
available from Gospel Light.

Safari Decorations

Send your guests on safari by using a few simple decorations. Hang an African print curtain at the entrance to the room. Decorate with African baskets, drums, pottery and other artifacts. Play traditional African music and set up a trading post in front of a life-sized backdrop. Hang travel posters and a map of Kenya or Africa on the walls. On a camp table, place a wildlife guide, survival guide, English-Swahili dictionary, binoculars, camera and canteen. Host or hostess dresses in khaki pants and shirt with hiking boots and safari hat, or a traditional African tribal costume from the Kenya area.

Use the clip art in this book to create the following safari party items:

- Wildlife name tags
- Safari brochure and wildlife guide
- Safari theme program

Also, use the clip art in this book to create the following life-sized safari wall decorations:

- Elephants, giraffes, zebras, rhinos, hippos
- Savannah scene with wildlife and traditional tribal homes
- Safari jeep or van

Safari Clip Art

Safari Snacks

Chapatis (African Bread)

Materials Checklist

- ☐ 2 c. whole wheat flour
- ☐ ½ tsp. salt
- ☐ 2 Tbs. vegetable oil plus extra for frying
- ☐ ½ c. water
- ☐ several rolling pins
- ☐ dish towel
- ☐ measuring cups
- ☐ measuring spoons
- ☐ pastry brush
- ☐ serving plate
- ☐ mixing bowl
- ☐ mixing spoon
- ☐ electric skillet
- ☐ cutting board
- ☐ spatula
- ☐ butter, cheese spread, peanut butter or honey butter
- ☐ paper plates
- ☐ knives

Serves 12.

Preparation: Set out all materials so children can see ingredients. Have children wash and dry hands.

Procedure: Children take turns completing the following tasks: Measure flour and salt into bowl. Mix 2 Tbs. of oil into the flour with hands. Stir in the water quickly and mix with hands until dough holds together. Knead the dough energetically on a lightly floured cutting board until it is smooth, about 5 minutes. Divide the dough into 12 balls. Keeping surface lightly floured, use rolling pins to flatten balls out to circles about 7 inches (17.5 cm) in diameter. Stack on serving plate and cover with dish towel to preserve freshness. One at a time and with adult supervision, brush oil onto one side of a chapati and place in skillet set at medium heat. Brown for a minute or so. Turn over with spatula and lightly brush oil on other side, brown for a minute or so. If chapati puffs up, press down gently with spatula. Serve to children on paper plates. Children then spread their chapatis with butter, cheese spread, peanut butter or honey butter.

Conversation: Ask, **What food do many people eat every day?** (Volunteers tell ideas.) **Different kinds of bread are eaten in many countries of the world every day. What are some different kinds of bread? Chapatis is a type of bread that is very common in Africa.**

Giraffe Salad

Materials Checklist

For each child—

☐ 1 medium stalk of celery cut to about 6 inches (15 cm) long

☐ peanut butter

☐ 1 Tbs. raisins

☐ 1 small pear half

☐ 1 dried apricot cut in half

☐ 2 sliced almonds

☐ kitchen knife

☐ measuring spoons

☐ paper plate

☐ plastic knife

☐ plastic fork

☐ napkin

Serves 1.

Preparation: Prepare a Giraffe Salad sample in advance for demonstration. Set out all materials so children can see ingredients. Wash celery and cut into 6-inch (15-cm) lengths. Cut apricots in half. Have children wash and dry hands.

Procedure: Each child places celery piece on a paper plate. Children use knives to spread peanut butter on the celery. Sprinkle raisins on the peanut butter to represent the spots on a giraffe's neck. Place the pear (cut side down) at one end of the celery neck, as the giraffe's head. Place the apricot halves at the top of the pear for the giraffe's ears. Place raisins on pear for eye and nose. Place almonds between apricots for horns.

almonds

pear half

dried apricot halves

raisins

peanut butter

celery

Zebra Melts

Materials Checklist

- ☐ 1 (1-lb.) box graham crackers
- ☐ 1 (13-oz.) bag white and dark striped chocolate kisses (Hershey Hugs candies without almonds)
- ☐ 1 (8-oz.) container of spreadable cream cheese
- ☐ plastic knives
- ☐ paper plates

Optional—

- ☐ 1 (24-oz.) squeeze bottle of chocolate sauce
- ☐ microwave with carousel

Serves 15.

Preparation: Set out all materials so children can see ingredients. Have children wash and dry hands.

Procedure: Each child places a whole graham cracker on paper plate. Then children place two unwrapped kisses on the crackers and put plates in direct sunlight for 10 minutes. (*Optional:* Use microwave with carousel continuously for 1 minute 40 seconds to melt chocolate.) Meanwhile, each child spreads cream cheese on another whole graham cracker. After the 10 minutes are up, children tap the softened kisses with knives. The kisses will spread out and form stripes. Top the "zebra"-striped crackers with the cream cheese crackers. (*Alternative:* Children spread cream cheese on graham crackers and squeeze chocolate sauce on the cream cheese to make zebra stripes.)

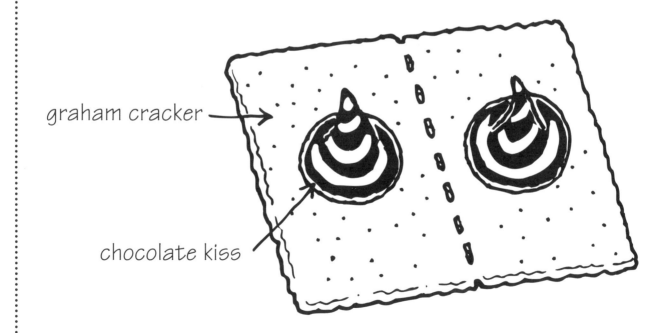

graham cracker

chocolate kiss

Hippo Coolers

Materials Checklist

- ☐ 1 or more blenders
- ☐ measuring cup
- ☐ kitchen knife
- ☐ paper cups
- ☐ plastic spoons
- ☐ napkins

For each child—

- ☐ 1 c. vanilla yogurt
- ☐ ½ nectarine or peach
- ☐ ½ banana
- ☐ 1 drop coconut extract
- ☐ 4 ice cubes

Serves 1.

Preparation: Set out all materials so children can see ingredients. Cut bananas and nectarines in half and peel. Have children wash and dry hands.

Procedure: Three children at a time may use blender to mix their drinks. Each child places his or her banana and nectarine in a blender with yogurt, coconut extract and ice cubes. Blend the drink about one minute or until most of the ice is crushed. Serve in paper cups with plastic spoons. Drink immediately.

Safari Snacks

Ndizi (Banana) Roll-Ups

Materials Checklist

- ☐ 1 (12-count) pkg. flour tortillas
- ☐ 1 (18-oz.) jar of peanut butter
- ☐ 12 bananas
- ☐ plastic knives
- ☐ napkins

Serves 12.

Preparation: Set out all materials so children can see ingredients. Have children wash and dry hands.

Procedure: Each child spreads peanut butter on a tortilla. (*Optional:* Use chapatis instead of tortillas.) Then each child peels a banana and rolls up the banana inside the tortilla.

Conversation: **Today we are going to make a snack called Ndizi Roll-Ups.** *Ndizi* **(n-deé-zee) is a Swahili word. Can anyone guess what it means?** (Banana.)

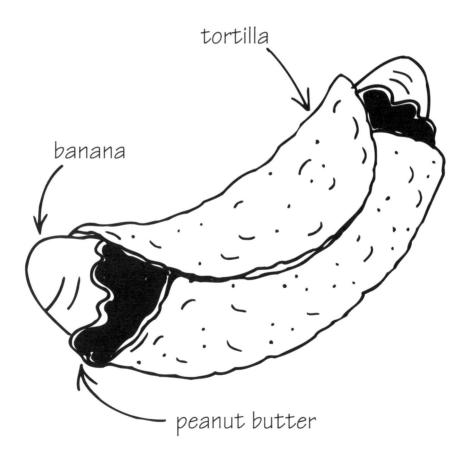

tortilla

banana

peanut butter

Baked Plantain or Bananas

Materials Checklist

- [ ] 8 large ripe bananas or plantains (washed)
- [ ] 1 c. brown sugar
- [ ] 1½ teaspoons cinnamon
- [ ] ½ c. melted butter or margarine
- [ ] knives
- [ ] small bowl
- [ ] mixing spoon
- [ ] measuring cups
- [ ] measuring spoons
- [ ] shallow baking pan
- [ ] aluminum foil
- [ ] small paper plates
- [ ] spoons

Serves 8.

Preparation: Set out all materials so children can see ingredients. Preheat oven to 350°. Have children wash and dry hands.

Procedure: Children slit each banana peel lengthwise and pull open slightly leaving a pocket for sugar mixture below. Arrange in a shallow baking pan with cut sides facing up.

In a small bowl, combine brown sugar, cinnamon and melted butter or margarine and stir well. Using spoon, pour brown sugar mixture over slit bananas. Cover pan with foil and bake for 20 minutes or until bananas are soft. Serve warm. Children use spoons to eat bananas out of their peels.

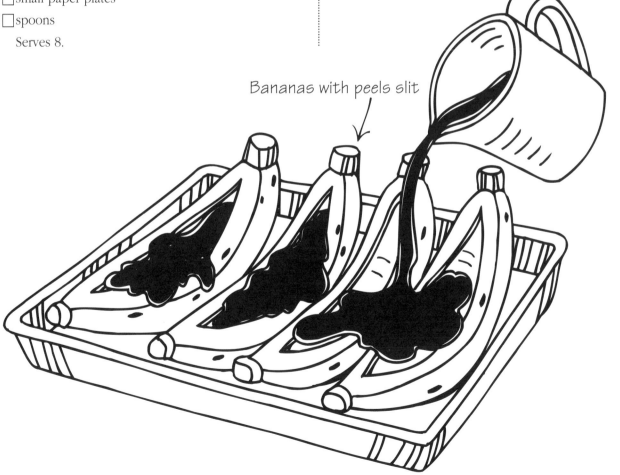

Bananas with peels slit

Safari Cutouts

Materials Checklist

☐ 1 (large) loaf of soft bread

☐ 1 (18-oz.) jar of spreadable peanut butter

☐ 1 (24-oz.) squeeze bottle of chocolate sauce

☐ 1 (8-oz.) container of spreadable cream cheese

☐ raisins

☐ chopped nuts

☐ candy sprinkles

☐ cookie cutters in zoo animal shapes

☐ plastic knives

☐ small bowls for sprinkles, nuts and raisins

Serves 20.

Preparation: Set out all materials so children can see ingredients. Place peanut butter, cream cheese, chocolate sauce and containers of sprinkles, nuts and raisins on table within reach of children. Have children wash and dry hands.

Procedure: Children use cookie cutters to cut animal shapes out of bread. (*Optional:* Younger children do not use cookie cutters. They decorate uncut slices of bread.) Children create animals. Giraffe can be made by spreading cutout with peanut butter and squeezing chocolate sauce in a grid design to create pattern. Create lion's mane with peanut butter, then sprinkles; make eyes and nose with raisins. Spread zebra with cream cheese and make stripes with chocolate sauce.

Apples on the Way

Materials Checklist

☐ peanut butter or cheese spread

☐ paring knife

☐ plastic knives

☐ napkins

For each child—

☐ 1 apple

Serves 1.

Preparation: Set out all materials so children can see ingredients. Have children wash and dry hands. Wash apples, then core with paring knife.

Procedure: Using plastic knife, child fills apple with cheese spread or peanut butter.

Safari Snacks

Banana Boats

Materials Checklist

- [ ] 8 large ripe bananas
- [ ] 1 (1-lb.) can crushed pineapple, drained
- [ ] 1 c. heavy whipping cream
- [ ] ¼ c. powdered sugar
- [ ] 1 tsp. vanilla
- [ ] 2 Tbs. brown sugar
- [ ] 1 c. chopped nuts
- [ ] measuring cups
- [ ] measuring spoons
- [ ] electric mixer
- [ ] paring knife
- [ ] 1 shallow mixing bowl
- [ ] 1 deep mixing bowl
- [ ] mixing spoon
- [ ] damp paper towels
- [ ] paper plates
- [ ] plastic spoons
- [ ] forks
- [ ] napkins

Serves 8.

Preparation: Set out all materials so children can see ingredients. Have children wash and dry hands. Wipe off the banana skins with a damp paper towel. Use paring knife to cut a 1-inch-wide (2.5 cm) strip along the entire length of outside curve of each banana.

Procedure: Children remove the banana-skin strips carefully and discard. Then they scoop out the fruit with a spoon, place in shallow mixing bowl and mash pulp with a fork. Stir in the pineapple. Place each banana skin on a paper plate and fill with the fruit mixture. Using an electric mixer set at high speed, whip the heavy cream and slowly add the powdered sugar, brown sugar and vanilla. Children top banana boats with the sweetened whipped cream and sprinkle with nuts. Serve immediately.

cut out a side section of peel

mixture of banana pulp and pineapple

whipped cream

Ostrich Egg Toss

Materials Checklist

☐ chalk, masking tape or rope

☐ measuring stick

For each team of four children—

☐ 1 white balloon (plus a few extras)

Preparation: Use chalk, masking tape or rope to mark off two lines 30 to 40 feet (9 to 12 m) apart. Inflate balloons.

Procedure: Each child chooses a partner. Assemble teams of four children, two pairs in a team. One pair in each team stands at one line and the other pair stands at the other line. Partners stand side by side and link arms. Give a balloon to each pair in one of the lines (see sketch). When the teacher says, "Go!" the partners hit the "ostrich egg" in the air with their free hands and try to keep it up as they run toward their teammates at the other line. If the balloon drops to the ground they may pick it up, but without unlinking arms. If the balloon pops, teacher provides a replacement. When each pair reaches their teammates, they hand the egg to them. Second pair hits the egg in the air as they run to the first line. The winners are the first team to complete the relay.

Lion's Cub

Materials Checklist

☐ a small stuffed or plastic lion

Procedure: Players sit in a semicircle. One player is selected to be the Lion. The Lion sits with eyes closed facing away from other players (see sketch). The Lion's Cub (toy lion) is placed directly behind the Lion. One at a time, players from the semicircle sneak up behind the Lion and try to take the Lion's Cub. If the Lion can hear the player approaching, he or she roars like a lion and that player sits down. If the Lion does not hear the player, that player takes the Lion's Cub and returns to his or her seat. The player hides the Lion's Cub behind him- or herself. The rest of the group then chants, "Lion, Lion, where is your cub?" The Lion turns around and has three chances to guess who has his Cub. If the Lion guesses incorrectly, the group says, "No!" If the Lion guesses correctly, the group applauds. The player with the Lion's Cub becomes the next Lion.

Catch the Tail

Procedure: Players line up one behind the other with their arms around the waists (or holding the shirts) of the players in front of them. The first player has his or her arms free. He or she tries to run and catch the last player in the line. The line twists and turns while the head of the line tries to catch the tail.

Anyone who lets go of the player in front is out. When the head of the line catches the tail, the player in front goes to the end of the line and the second person becomes the head. Continue playing until everyone has had a turn to be the head.

Hiking Boot Relay

Materials Checklist

☐ 4 to 8 large paper bags

☐ 2 to 4 chairs

☐ chalk

☐ measuring stick

Optional—

☐ safari hats, gloves and/or large jackets

Preparation: Use chalk to draw a starting line. For each team, place a chair 20 feet (6 m) away from the starting line.

Procedure: Divide group into teams. Each team lines up behind the starting line. Give the first player on each team two paper bags. At the signal, players put paper bags on their feet as boots, run carefully to the chairs, pass behind them and return to their lines. They take off their boots and give them to the second players, who don the boots and repeat the process. The first player on each team goes to the end of his or her line. Continue playing until all members on each team have had a turn. The boots will be much the worse for wear. However, each child *must* run around the chair and back with the boots on his or her feet. (*Optional:* Players put on additional safari wear such as hats, gloves and/or jackets.)

Safari Stampede

Materials Checklist

☐ a soft rubber ball or sponge

☐ measuring stick

    Procedure: Divide group into four teams. Give each team the name of a safari animal (Giraffe, Elephant, Zebra, Rhinoceros). The teams line up along opposite sides of an open area at least 20 yards (18 m) square.

Choose one player to be the "Lion." The Lion stands between the teams and calls out the names of two of the "animals." (Example: Giraffes, Rhinos.) The Giraffes and the Rhinos run to exchange places with each other. The Lion tries to capture one of the animals by throwing a soft rubber ball or sponge at him or her. The captured animal then becomes the Lion.

Variation: Players who get hit by the ball are out. Last player to get hit becomes the new Lion.

Safari Games•**Middler**

Backpack Stuff

Materials Checklist

☐ 2 sturdy backpacks of equal size

☐ miscellaneous camping or
   safari items of various sizes

☐ pencil and paper for scoring

☐ solid-colored stickers

☐ felt pen

☐ masking tape

☐ measuring stick

Preparation: Use stickers or masking tape to label each camping item with a certain number of points. The greater the survival need, the higher the points. (For example: water=200 points, CD player=5 points.) Place camping items in one big pile. Use masking tape to mark a starting line. Place backpacks about 20 feet (6 m) from starting line.

Procedure: Divide class into two teams and have them line up on starting line. The object of the game is for each team to pack its backpack with items that have the most points. First player from each team takes an item from the pile, then runs to his or her team's backpack. Player puts the item in the backpack, then runs back and tags the next person in line. If the item does not fit into the backpack, the player must take that item back to the pile. If by removing one item the player can get his or her item to fit, he or she may return the removed item to the pile. Only one item at a time may be taken from the pile and carried. Dropped items are eliminated from the game. Game continues until every player has had a turn. At end of game, each backpack is unpacked and the points are tallied. The team with the highest number of points wins.

20 feet

African Snake Game

Materials Checklist

☐ chalk

☐ several socks

☐ measuring stick

Preparation: Use chalk to make a large circle on the pavement, approximately 10 feet (3 m) in diameter. Letter the word "Home" in the center of the circle. Stuff sock with several other socks to use for a "snake."

Procedure: (Establish boundaries.) Children stand outside circle. One child claps hands or stomps feet, while the other children pass the snake to each other. When the child stops clapping or stomping, the person who has the snake chases the other children, who try to avoid the snake. If a child is tagged by the snake, he or she must hold hands with the player holding the snake. As the snake grows, these players work together to capture the others by encircling or cornering runners. If the snake chain breaks apart, the players in the chain must run back to Home to reassemble. The game ends when time is called or when everyone is part of the snake.

Lion, Lion

Materials Checklist

☐ chalk

☐ measuring stick

Preparation: Use chalk to draw a large square about 10×10 feet (3×3 m). Letter the word "Den" inside the square. Draw a safety line 20-30 feet (6-9 m) away from the Den.

Procedure: Choose one child to be the Lion. This child stands in the Den and closes his or her eyes, pretending to be asleep. The other children run up to the Den and whisper, "Lion, lion are you sleeping?" The Lion stays asleep. Then the children say in a normal voice, "Lion, lion are you sleeping?" The Lion stays asleep. Finally the children yell, "Lion, lion are you sleeping?" This time the Lion chases the children from the Den to the safety line. Any children who cross the safety line before the Lion tags them are safe. Any children the Lion tags come back to the Den with the Lion and become Lion Cubs. The children who crossed the safety line repeat the questions as before to the Lion who again pretends to be asleep. This time, after the children yell, the Lion and Cubs chase and tag children. This process continues until all the children have been caught. The last child caught by a Lion or Cub becomes the new Lion and game begins again.

The Big Book of Theme Parties, Snacks and Games © 1997 by Gospel Light. Permission to photocopy granted.

Animal Adventure

Materials Checklist

☐ enough chairs for all but two of the players

Preparation: Place chairs in a double row, back to back (as in Musical Chairs).

Procedure: Divide group into pairs. Each pair decides on an "animal" it will be and links arms. (For example, a pair of Lions, a pair of Zebras, a pair of Elephants, etc.) All players, except one pair that is "It," sit in chairs. "It" walks around saying the names of various animals. When a pair's animal name is called, the pair stands and follows "It," walking in a way that resembles their animal. If "It" says "The animals are quiet tonight," all the players join the line. If "It" says, "The animals are restless tonight," everyone runs for seats. The pair left without seats becomes the new "It."

Jump and Run Relay

Materials Checklist

☐ 2 small squares of African-print fabric for flags

☐ masking tape, rope or chalk

☐ measuring stick

Preparation: Use masking tape, rope or chalk to draw two lines 20-30 feet (6-9 m) apart.

Group children into two even teams. Both teams line up behind starting line. Give a flag to the first player on each team. When the teacher shouts, "Go!" the first player on each team does a standing broad jump, then hops on one foot to the opposite line. Player then runs back to his or her team, passing the flag to the next person in line, who continues the relay. When the last person on a team completes the relay, his or her team sits down.

Safari Games • Junior
Trail the Tail

Materials Checklist

☐ 6 tube socks

Preparation: Tie the ends of three socks together to make a "tail." Make two tails.

Procedure: Divide group into two teams. Teams line up, holding on to each other's wrists. The last child in each line tucks a tail in his or her waistband.

At teacher's signal, the first child leads his or her team around the playing area trying to snatch the tail from the other team. At the same time, the last child tries to move so that his or her team's tail will not be snatched. If a team's line is broken, the team must stop until all wrists are held again. First team to snatch a tail is the winner.

Canoe Race

Materials Checklist

☐ scissors

☐ string

☐ small waxed paper cups

Preparation: Punch a hole in center bottom of each cup.

Procedure: Divide group into teams of four to six players and arrange each team in a line with players standing side by side. Give each team a paper cup and a length of string that reaches the length of the line. The first player threads the cup onto the string with bottom towards next player. At a given signal, with the string held taut, the first player begins blowing into the cup, sending it to the next player. Each player continues racing the "canoe" on its way to the end of the line by blowing cup to the next player in line. The first team to propel its canoe to the end of the line wins.

Safari Stepping-Stones

Materials Checklist

☐ masking tape or rope

☐ measuring stick

For each team—

☐ two 16-inch (40-cm) squares of heavy cloth or carpet samples

Preparation: Use masking tape or rope to mark goal line 30 feet (9 m) from starting area.

Procedure: Divide group into teams of four to six players and have each team form a line. Give the first player in each line two squares of cloth or carpet. At a given signal, the first player on each team places one square on the ground in front of him or her, then jumps on it. While standing on the first square, player places the second square a few feet ahead and jumps onto it. Player then reaches back, picks up the first square and places it ahead. The players continue this procedure, making sure feet do not touch ground, until goal line is reached. Then player picks up squares, runs back to team and hands squares to next player, who follows the same procedure. Continue playing until all players on one team have had a turn.

30 feet

Goal Line

Safari Games • Junior
Cheetah Pounce

Materials Checklist

☐ masking tape or rope

☐ measuring stick

For each team—

☐ a large ball

Preparation: Use masking tape or rope to make a goal line 30 feet (9 m) away from starting line.

Procedure: Divide group into even teams, with six or fewer players to a team. Have each team form a line in a large playing area. Give each team a ball. The first player on each team places the ball between his or her knees and runs (or hops) to a goal line. Crossing the line, the player grabs the ball and runs back to the team, hands it to the next player, who places it between knees and hops toward goal line. Continue in relay fashion until everyone on the team has run.

Tropical Island

Theme craft ideas can be found in the
Treasure Chest of Crafts book,
available from Gospel Light.

Tropical Island Decorations

An enchanting tropical island can be portrayed with a few simple decorations. Hang strings of clear blue and green beads over the entrance to your room and play a cassette tape of rain forest sounds as guests enter. Place potted ferns, palms, hibiscus or other colorful blooming plants around. Hang maps and travel posters of tropical islands and a treasure map on the walls. Play island music on a cassette player. Place an ocean canoe or raft with oars in a corner. Display island print tablecloths, fishnet with shells and fish, beach umbrellas, toys and towels. Fill baskets with pineapples, bananas, mangos and papayas. Use electric fans placed behind plants or fishnet and a well-placed jasmine room deodorizer to create a scented island breeze. Host or hostess dresses in island print clothing.

Use the clip art in this book to create the following island party items:

- Island animal and sea life name tags
- Island theme invitations
- Island theme programs
- Island guide or brochure

Also, use clip art to create the following life-sized island wall decorations:

- Underwater scene with dolphins and other sea life
- Sand castles on the shore
- Tropical lagoon with palm trees

The Big Book of Theme Parties, Snacks and Games © 1997 by Gospel Light. Permission to photocopy granted.

167

Tropical Island Clip Art

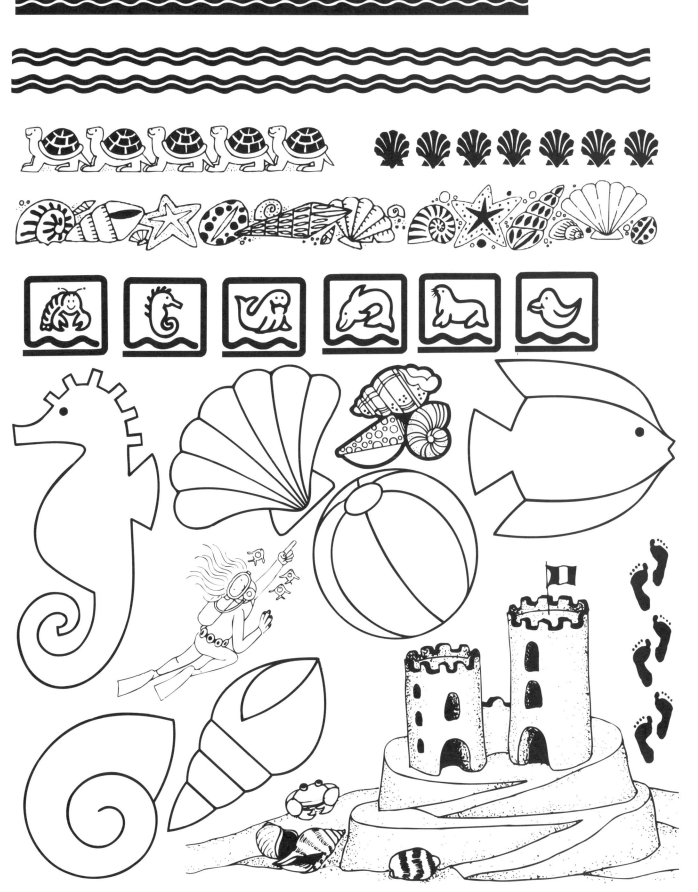

Tropical Island Snacks

Frozen Bananas

Materials Checklist

- ☐ 4 small bananas
- ☐ 2 (8-oz.) containers of flavored yogurt
- ☐ chopped nuts, flaked coconut or granola
- ☐ paper plates
- ☐ 8 popsicle sticks
- ☐ plastic wrap
- ☐ napkins
- ☐ knives

Serves 8.

Preparation: Cut bananas in half and insert a popsicle stick into cut end. Wrap bananas with plastic wrap and freeze. Place yogurt and chopped nuts, flaked coconut or granola on paper plates. Set out all materials so children can see all ingredients. Have children wash and dry hands.

Procedure: Children roll their bananas in yogurt, then in chopped nuts, coconut or granola.

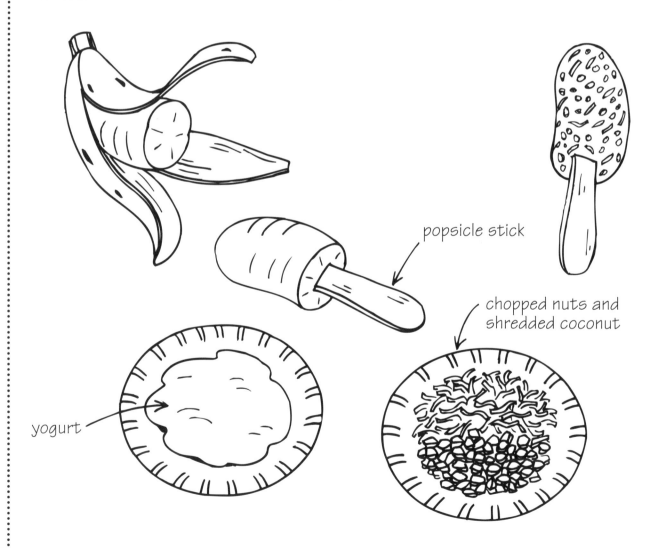

popsicle stick

chopped nuts and shredded coconut

yogurt

Tropical Fruit Bowl

Materials Checklist

- [ ] ½ watermelon
- [ ] 1 cantaloupe
- [ ] 1 honeydew melon
- [ ] 1 (7-oz.) pkg. flaked coconut
- [ ] cutting board
- [ ] kitchen knife
- [ ] mixing bowl
- [ ] mixing spoon
- [ ] small paper cups
- [ ] plastic forks
- [ ] napkins

Serves 12-15.

Preparation: Cut fruit into bite-sized chunks. Mix chunks of watermelon, cantaloupe and honeydew with flaked coconut. Have children wash and dry hands.

Procedure: Place fruit in small paper cups with forks and serve to children.

Island Fizz

Materials Checklist

- [ ] 1 (2-liter) bottle soda water
- [ ] 1 (12-oz.) can frozen tropical fruit juice concentrate
- [ ] crushed ice
- [ ] paper cups
- [ ] pitcher
- [ ] mixing spoon
- [ ] napkins

Preparation: In pitcher, mix soda water with fruit juice concentrate. Have children wash and dry hands.

Procedure: Place crushed ice in paper cups. Pour juice mixture over crushed ice in paper cups and serve to children.

crushed ice

Banana Wafers

Materials Checklist

- ☐ 4 bananas
- ☐ 1 (12-oz.) box vanilla wafers
- ☐ plastic knives
- ☐ cutting boards
- ☐ paper plates
- ☐ napkins

  Serves 10-15.

Preparation: Prepare a Banana Wafer sample in advance for demonstration. Set out all materials so children can see all ingredients. Have children wash and dry hands.

Procedure: Children peel and slice bananas. Then they place a slice of banana between two vanilla wafers and enjoy.

Tropical Island Snacks

Orange Squizzles

Materials Checklist

For each child—

☐ ½ orange

☐ 1 peppermint or cinnamon candy stick

☐ kitchen knife

☐ paper plate

☐ napkin

Preparation: Prepare an Orange Squizzle sample in advance for demonstration. Set out all materials so children can see all ingredients. Peel wrappers from candy sticks and break in half. Have children wash and dry hands.

Procedure: Children soften oranges by rolling between their hands. Teacher then collects oranges, cuts them in half and returns half an orange to each child. Children then push their peppermint or cinnamon candy stick halves into center of their orange halves which may then be used as a straw.

Beachcomber's Snack

Materials Checklist

- ☐ 3 c. mini Shredded Wheat squares
- ☐ ¼ c. melted margarine
- ☐ 1 c. pretzel sticks
- ☐ 1 c. fish-shaped crackers
- ☐ 1 c. oyster crackers
- ☐ ½ c. grated Parmesan cheese
- ☐ salt to taste
- ☐ mixing bowl
- ☐ measuring cups
- ☐ mixing spoon
- ☐ cookie sheet
- ☐ paper plates
- ☐ napkins

Serves 10-12.

Preparation: Set out all materials so children can see ingredients. Have children wash and dry hands.

Procedure: Pour mini Shredded Wheat squares and melted margarine into a bowl and mix together. Add pretzel sticks and crackers. Sprinkle on grated Parmesan cheese and salt. Stir contents together and spread on a cookie sheet. Bake for 5 minutes at 350°. Serve warm.

wheat squares

pretzel sticks

fish-shaped crackers

salt

oyster crackers

melted butter

Parmesan cheese

Java Dessert (Coffee Slushee)

Materials Checklist

☐ 2 c. milk

☐ 1 Tbs. instant decaffeinated coffee

☐ 3 Tbs. sugar

☐ bag of ice cubes

☐ measuring cups and spoons

☐ paper cups

☐ straws

☐ blender

Optional—

☐ 2 tsp. vanilla

☐ 1 tsp. cinnamon

☐ 1 (7-oz.) can of whipped cream

Serves 8.

Preparation: Set out all materials so children can see ingredients. Have children wash and dry hands.

Procedure: With adult supervision, children pour 2 cups of milk into blender, then add ice to fill. Children take turns measuring coffee and sugar into the blender. Blend until thick and frothy. Pour into cups. (*Optional:* Add cinnamon and vanilla to mixture in blender. Top with whipped cream.) Drink immediately.

Tropical Island Snacks

"Down in the Sea" Cups

Materials Checklist

- ☐ 2 large pkgs. blue JELL-O
- ☐ Gummy Fish
- ☐ 1 (8-oz.) small tub of nondairy whipped topping
- ☐ boiling water
- ☐ cold water
- ☐ saucepan
- ☐ measuring cups
- ☐ ice cubes
- ☐ wooden spoon
- ☐ refrigerator
- ☐ plastic pitcher
- ☐ clear (9-ounce) plastic cups
- ☐ plastic spoons

    Serves 12.

Preparation: Boil water. Set out all materials so children see ingredients. Have children wash and dry hands.

Procedure: In pitcher, children mix JELL-O according to package directions for speed-set method using boiling water, cold water and ice cubes. Allow children to take turns stirring until ice melts. Each child puts a few Gummy Fish into a plastic cup. Pour liquid JELL-O over fish to fill each cup three-fourths full. Place cups in the refrigerator for 30 minutes. When JELL-O has set, children can spoon some whipped topping "waves" onto the top of their JELL-O "sea."

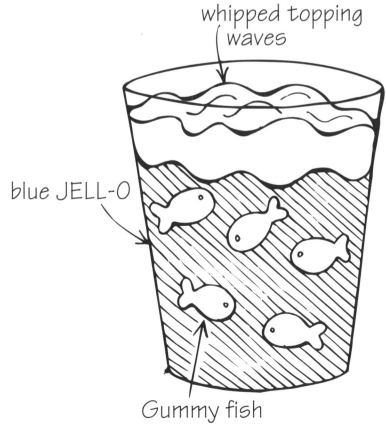

whipped topping waves

blue JELL-O

Gummy fish

Melon Boats

Materials Checklist

☐ melons such as cantaloupe
☐ blueberries, strawberries or grapes
☐ American cheese slices cut diagonally
☐ long pretzel sticks
☐ knife
☐ cutting board
☐ toothpicks
☐ napkins
☐ paper plates

Preparation: Slice one wedge of melon for each child. Set out all materials so children can see ingredients. Have children wash and dry hands.

Procedure: Children use pretzel to make a "mast" in melon wedge. Then children add cheese "sails," securing with toothpicks (see sketch). Children make "sailors" by slipping fruit onto toothpicks and sticking toothpicks into melon.

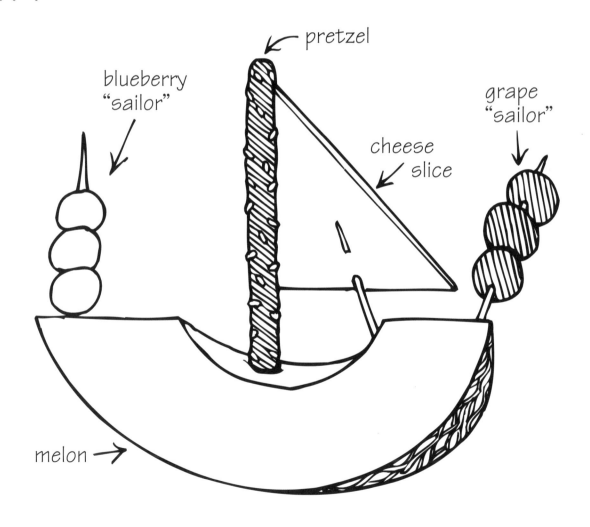

Fish-Face Sandwiches

Materials Checklist

☐ 1 large loaf sliced wheat bread

☐ green olives with pimento slices

☐ tuna salad

☐ mayonnaise

☐ bread knives

☐ paper plates

Optional—

☐ peanut butter

☐ apple or grape jelly

Preparation: Set out all materials so children can see ingredients. Have children wash and dry hands.

Procedure: Give each child a paper plate, two slices of bread and a bread knife. Children cut bread to make two fish shapes (see sketch). Children spread tuna salad onto the bottom slice of bread. Then they place other slice of bread on top. Use a little mayonnaise to secure an olive slice to the top slice of bread to make a fish eye.

(*Optional:* Children spread peanut butter and jelly on the bottom slice of their sandwiches to make "jelly fish" sandwiches.)

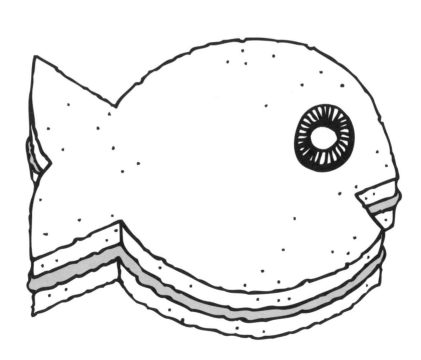

Sleeping Sea Turtles

Procedure: Choose one player to be the hunter. The rest of the players are the sea turtles. As the hunter counts slowly to ten, the turtles lie down and pretend to be asleep. When finished counting, the hunter carefully watches all the turtles to try to catch one of them moving. Any that are caught moving must join the hunter and help watch the rest of the turtles. The turtle that stays motionless the longest is "king of the island."

Tropical Island Games • **Primary**

Pineapple Toss

Materials Checklist
- [ ] large triangular piece of cardboard
- [ ] felt pens
- [ ] masking tape
- [ ] paper and pencil for scoring
- [ ] bean bag

Procedure: With felt pen draw six pineapples on cardboard. Number the pineapples. Place cardboard on the floor and mark a line with masking tape a few yards (meters) in front of it, behind which the players stand. Players take turns tossing bean bag onto pineapples. (Score is determined by the number in the pineapple.) After each player has had several turns, the player with the highest score is the winner.

Tropical Island Games•**Primary**

Stuck in the Sand

Procedure: Choose one player to be "It." Children run and try to avoid being tagged by "It." Any player tagged by "It" is "stuck in the sand" and has to stand still with legs apart and call for help. Any player not yet tagged can free him or her by crawling between his or her legs. Keep playing until there is only one player not "stuck in the sand."

Tropical Island Games • **Primary**

Volcano!

Procedure: Choose a child to be "It." Divide remaining group into two even teams. If teams are uneven, a teacher or aide joins a team to balance the numbers. Team A forms a circle. "It" stands in the center of the circle. Each member of Team B stands behind one of the members of Team A (see sketch). "It" starts clapping, which signals that the "volcano" is erupting. The inside circle, Team A, claps with "It" and Team B runs clockwise around the circle. When "It" stops clapping, Team A stops clapping too. "It" and Team B members each run to stand behind a member of Team A. The player left without someone to stand behind is the next "It." Team A and Team B change places before the game begins again.

Sharks and Squids

Materials Checklist

☐ masking tape or rope

Preparation: Use masking tape or rope to make two goal lines.

Procedure: Divide group into two equal teams— the Sharks and the Squids. Each group stands at opposite ends of the play area. The Sharks turn their backs and stand on their goal line. The leader watches the Squids sneak up on them. When leader thinks they are near enough, he or she calls, "The Squids are coming!" The Sharks turn around and chase the Squids back to the Squid goal line. Any Squids who are caught count as points for the Sharks. Then the Squids turn their backs while the Sharks sneak up on them. When the leader calls, "The Sharks are coming!" the Squids turn and chase the Sharks back to the Shark goal. Any Sharks who are caught count as points for the Squids. The group having the most points at the end of playing time wins.

The Big Book of Theme Parties, Snacks and Games © 1997 by Gospel Light. Permission to photocopy granted.

Porpoise Partners

Materials Checklist

For each player—

☐ a 10-inch (25-cm) piece of yarn

Procedure: Divide into two equal groups. Group 1 forms a circle with everyone facing out. Group 2 forms an outer circle facing Group 1. Players join hands with the person in the other circle whom they are facing. Partners drop hands, then those in inner circle march, skip or slide counterclockwise while outer circle moves in opposite direction around the circle (sketch a.) When leader shouts, "Porpoise partners," each player must run to find his or her partner, join hands and sit down. The last two players to sit down must each tie a piece of yarn around his or her wrist (sketch b.) Repeat this procedure until only two children are left without yarn on a wrist.

Island Relay

<u>Materials Checklist</u>

☐ small beach balls

Procedure: Divide into two or more equal teams. Each team forms a line, one player behind the other, with legs spread apart. The first player on each team holds ball and bends over at waist. When leader says, "Go," the balls are rolled between players' legs to the person at the end of each line. The last person picks up the ball and runs to the beginning of his or her line and repeats procedure. Continue until one team completes the relay.

The Great Snack Search

Materials Checklist

☐ at least one Styrofoam ice chest containing a water-melon

☐ shovel or other digging tools

☐ a large area with soft dirt or sand (a beach or a ploughed field)

Optional—

☐ small snack items

☐ index cards

☐ felt pen

Preparation: Bury and camouflage the ice chest(s).

Procedure: Divide group into two or more teams. Turn them loose in the designated area to try to uncover the buried treasure(s). They can dig with hands or any implements available. When the treasure is found, cut up the watermelon as the snack for the day.

Options:

1. Hide a number of small snack items. Each team's job is to make sure all their team members get a snack.

2. On index cards write clues to where the hidden treasure can be found. You may have teams search for the same treasure, or send each team off to find a different one.

Bridge the Gap

Materials Checklist

☐ a large, grassy playing area

Procedure: Divide group into teams of three players. Player 1 on each team lies facedown on the ground. Player 2 straddles player 1, runs the length of player 1 and lies down. Player 1 then grabs the ankles of player 2. Player 3 straddles player 1, runs the length of both players on the ground and lies down. Player 2 grabs his or her ankles. Player 1 then stands up and runs. Continue end-over-end until one team has reached a designated finish line.

Tropical Island Games • **Junior**

Sea Horse Tag

Materials Checklist

☐ a large, grassy playing area

Procedure: Select three players to start the game, one of whom is "It." The remaining children form pairs and stand side by side with arms interlocked. "It" chases the two unpaired players among the group of paired children. Any player being chased may run and interlock arms with one of the other players to avoid being tagged. The player on the opposite end of the newly-formed trio must now let go and run, being chased by "It." As a player is tagged he or she becomes "It" and begins chasing others not joined to a partner. Game ends when designated time is up.

Tropical Island Games • **Junior**

Island Ball

Materials Checklist

☐ beach ball

☐ wooden or plastic bat or stick

☐ 5 pieces of cardboard or carpet squares

Procedure: Divide group into two teams. Lay pieces of cardboard or carpet in a baseball-diamond shape on the ground. Commence playing ball following regular softball rules.

Variation: A game of kickball may also be played using the beach ball instead of a regular ball.

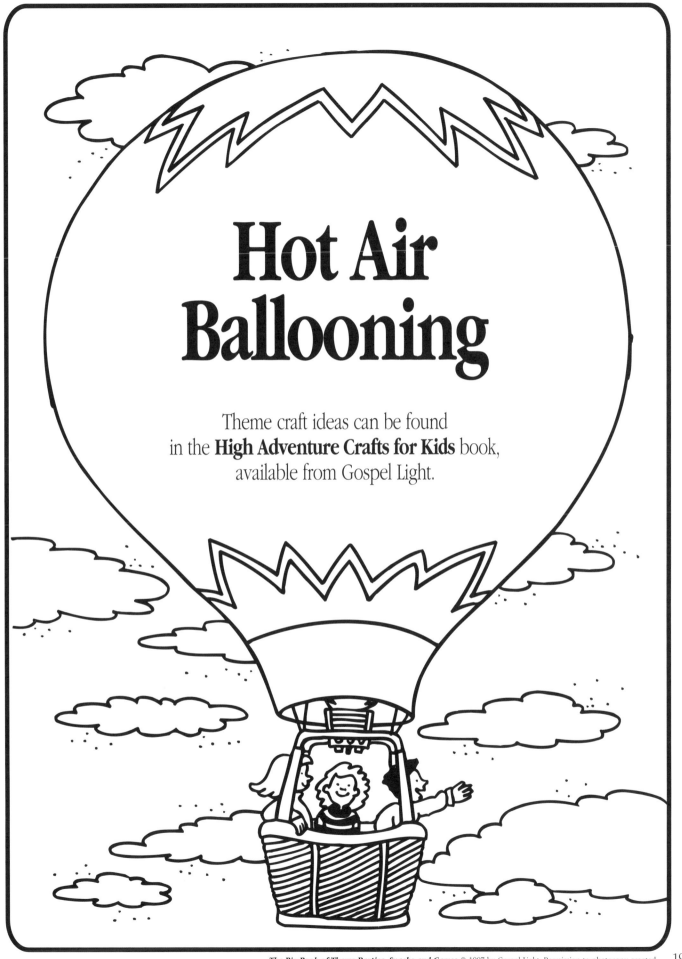

Hot Air Ballooning

Theme craft ideas can be found
in the **High Adventure Crafts for Kids** book,
available from Gospel Light.

Hot Air Ballooning Decorations

Take your guests up in the air by using a few simple decorations. Hang hot air balloon posters on the walls. Decorate helium balloons by attaching strawberry baskets with string to resemble hot air balloons. Create a life-sized gondola with a large furniture or appliance box. Color or paint instruments, fuel container and ballast on the box. Set gondola in front of a blue butcher paper backdrop on which a hot air balloon has been painted. Then hang fiberfill from the ceiling to create clouds.

Use the clip art in this book to create the following ballooning party items:
- Hot air balloon name tags
- Invitations
- Balloon rally programs
- Ballooning terms

Also, use the clip art in this book to create the following life-sized ballooning wall decorations:
- Hot air balloons in the sky with scenery of the land below
- Balloon rally event

Hot Air Ballooning Clip Art

Up and Away

Hot Air Ballooning Snacks

Rice Cake Balloons

Materials Checklist

☐ 1 pkg. rice cakes (12-14)

☐ 1 (16-ounce) tub cream cheese, softened

☐ food coloring

☐ black olives, sliced (5 oz.)

☐ green olives, sliced (5 oz.)

☐ knives

☐ 6 bowls

☐ spoons

☐ small paper plates

For every two children—

☐ 1 slice bologna

Serves 12-14.

Preparation: Set out all materials so children can see ingredients. Place black and green olives in bowls. Spoon cream cheese into four of the bowls. Have children wash and dry hands.

Procedure: Children stir food coloring into bowls containing cream cheese to make various colors. Children spread colored cream cheese on their rice cakes to make hot air balloon designs. Children cut bologna into narrow strips, triangles and other shapes. Then they decorate their balloons using strips of bologna and olives (see sketch).

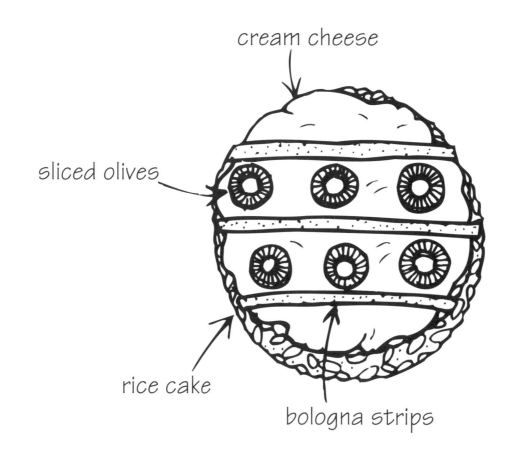

cream cheese

sliced olives

rice cake

bologna strips

JELL-O Hot Air Balloons

Materials Checklist

☐ 3 large pkgs. of JELL-O in a variety of bright colors

☐ 1 (10-oz.) pkg. of Lorna Doone®
  (or other square) cookies

☐ red or black licorice laces

☐ round cookie cutter, approximately 3 inches
  (7.5 cm) in diameter

☐ boiling water

☐ measuring cups

☐ saucepan

☐ mixing bowls

☐ mixing spoons

☐ 3 8-inch (20-cm) square pans

☐ refrigerator

☐ knife

☐ paper plates

Optional—

☐ Gummy Bears or Teddy Grahams
  Serves 12.

Preparation: Make various colors of JELL-O Jigglers by mixing each large package of JELL-O with 1¼ cup boiling water. Pour into pans and allow to set in refrigerator overnight. Dip bottom of pan in warm water about 15 seconds. Use cookie cutter to cut JELL-O into circles—one for each child. Cut each circle into three sections (see sketch). Set out all materials so children can see ingredients. Have children wash and dry hands.

Procedure: Each child chooses three colored JELL-O sections to form a circle and fits them together on a paper plate to create a hot air balloon. Then children break pieces of licorice to form ropes from the balloon to a gondola, which is made with a square cookie. (*Optional:* Children may add Gummy Bears or Teddy Grahams to ride in their gondolas.)

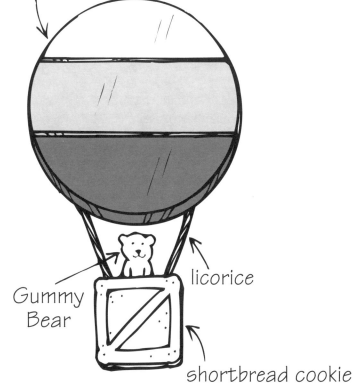

JELL-O shapes fitted together

Gummy
Bear

licorice

shortbread cookie

Map Cookies

Materials Checklist

- ☐ 1 small pkg. chocolate chips
- ☐ 1 (12-ounce) can evaporated milk
- ☐ food coloring in a variety of colors
- ☐ blue and green candy sprinkles
- ☐ flaked coconut
- ☐ container of cinnamon-sugar
- ☐ one baking sheet for every 3-4 children
- ☐ empty margarine tub
- ☐ small paper cups
- ☐ water color paintbrushes
- ☐ knife
- ☐ can opener
- ☐ heavy-duty foil
- ☐ permanent felt pen
- ☐ wet paper towels for clean-up
- ☐ paper plates

For every 8 children—

- ☐ 2 pkgs. premade sugar-cookie dough

Serves 8.

Preparation: Set out all materials so children can see ingredients. Pour chocolate chips into margarine tub. Tear or cut foil into 8-inch (20-cm) lengths—one for each child. Preheat oven to 350°. Have children wash and dry hands.

Procedure: Give each child a foil piece and one-fourth of the premade cookie dough. Child uses felt pen to letter name on foil and presses the dough into desired shape on foil to make map base. Children pour a small amount of evaporated milk into paper cups and use paintbrush to mix one color of food coloring into each. Children paint features on their cookie map with the evaporated milk paint. Then they may use chocolate chips for mountain peaks, colored sprinkles for lakes, rivers or forested areas, flaked coconut for snow and cinnamon-sugar for dirt areas. Place maps (on foil pieces) on ungreased baking sheets. Bake according to package directions. (Cookies may take several minutes longer due to their size.)

Conversation: Ask, **What might you see from up high in a hot air balloon?** (Volunteers respond.) **Today you can make a map from cookie dough. Your map will look like you're high in the air.**

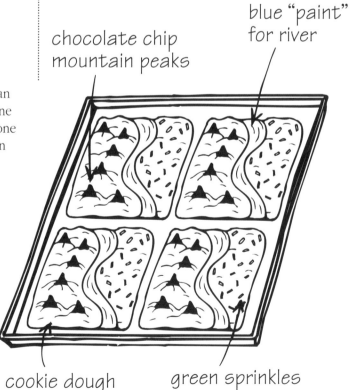

chocolate chip mountain peaks

blue "paint" for river

cookie dough

green sprinkles

Hot Air Balloon Rolls

Materials Checklist

- [ ] 2 pkgs. (24-roll pkg.) frozen dinner-rolls dough
- [ ] 1 (1-pound) pkg. large marshmallows
- [ ] 1 cube melted butter or margarine
- [ ] sugar sprinkles in several colors
- [ ] 4 baking sheets
- [ ] several small bowls
- [ ] small saucepan
- [ ] foil
- [ ] small paper plates
- [ ] kitchen towels
- [ ] permanent felt pen

Serves 24 (2 rolls apiece).

Preparation: Thaw dinner rolls (approximately one hour). Melt butter in saucepan. Pour into one bowl. Pour colored sprinkles into small bowls. Tear foil into 5-inch (12.5-cm) lengths—one for each child. Set out all materials so children can see ingredients. Have children wash and dry hands.

Procedure: Give each child a foil piece, two thawed dinner rolls and two marshmallows. Child uses felt pen to letter name on foil. Children place rolls on foil, pressing and stretching them into 4-inch (10-cm) circles. Then they place a marshmallow in the center of their circles and pinch the dough tightly around the marshmallow. Children dip rolls into the melted butter to coat top of roll. Then they dip the top of the roll into one color of sprinkles. Children repeat, dipping the opposite half of roll in a different color. Place rolls (on foil pieces) on ungreased baking sheets about 2 inches (5 cm) apart. Cover rolls with towels and let rise in unheated oven until double in size and puffy, approximately 45 minutes. Then bake at 375° for 20-25 minutes or until golden brown. Allow rolls to cool 15 minutes, then serve on paper plates. When children pull open these buns they will find them hollow, with only hot air inside!

Sunny Sky Dessert Cup

Materials Checklist

- [ ] 2 large pkgs. blue JELL-O
- [ ] vanilla wafers
- [ ] yellow decorator icing in squeeze tube
- [ ] 1 (12-oz.) tub of nondairy whipped topping
- [ ] boiling water
- [ ] cold water
- [ ] ice cubes
- [ ] saucepan
- [ ] measuring cup
- [ ] mixing bowl
- [ ] mixing spoon
- [ ] 12 (9-oz.) clear plastic cups
- [ ] plastic spoons

Serves 12.

Preparation: Boil water. Set out all materials so children can see ingredients. Have children wash and dry hands.

Procedure: Mix JELL-O according to package directions for speed-set method using boiling water, cold water and ice cubes. Refrigerate until gelatin is thick enough to mound slightly. Spoon thickened gelatin into plastic cups, alternating with spoonfuls of whipped topping placed around the sides of plastic cup to form clouds. Refrigerate for one hour until set.

Children use yellow decorator icing to make a sun on a vanilla wafer. Then they top gelatin with a spoonful of whipped topping and place their "sun" cookie peeking out from the "cloud."

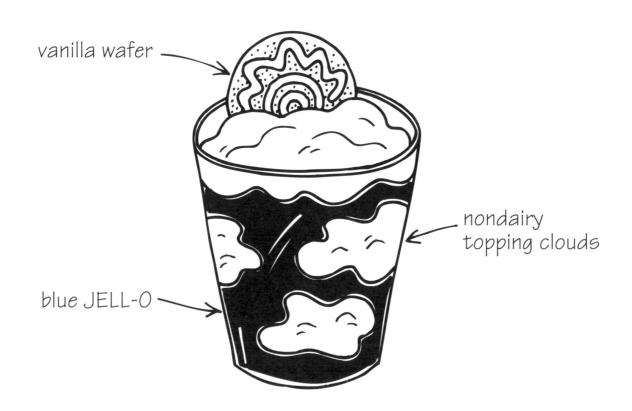

vanilla wafer

nondairy topping clouds

blue JELL-O

Get Up and Go Smoothie

Materials Checklist

- ☐ 1 c. milk
- ☐ 1 (6-oz.) can frozen juice concentrate
- ☐ 2 c. vanilla ice cream
- ☐ blender
- ☐ ice cream scoop
- ☐ 9-oz. paper cups
- ☐ 6 drinking straws
- ☐ measuring cup

    Serves 6.

Preparation: Set out all materials so children can see ingredients. Have children wash and dry hands.

Procedure: Pour the juice concentrate and milk into a blender. Add 2 cups vanilla ice cream. Blend for 20 seconds. Pour into cups and serve with straws.

Pink Egg Balloons

Materials Checklist

- ☐ 4 eggs
- ☐ 1 can julienne beets
- ☐ 3 slices ham or other luncheon meat
- ☐ 3 slices processed cheese
- ☐ 2 carrots
- ☐ 1 box soda or Triscuit crackers
- ☐ 1 Tbs. mayonnaise
- ☐ ½ tsp. mustard
- ☐ water
- ☐ measuring spoons
- ☐ can opener
- ☐ saucepan
- ☐ 2 paper or plastic cups
- ☐ mixing bowl
- ☐ knives
- ☐ fork
- ☐ cutting board
- ☐ paper towels
- ☐ plastic spoons
- ☐ plastic forks
- ☐ paper plates

Serves 8.

Preparation: Hard boil eggs in saucepan. Drain beet juice into cups, dividing juice evenly. Cut carrots into 1 to 2-inch (2.5 to 5-cm) thin strips. Set out all materials so children can see ingredients. Have children wash and dry hands.

Procedure: Remove shells from hard-boiled eggs and cut eggs in half lengthwise. Scoop out the yolks into a mixing bowl. Immerse each egg white half into a cup of beet juice for one minute. (Eggs will not taste like beets.) Remove and turn upside down on a paper towel placed on a paper plate. Mix egg yolks with the mayonnaise and mustard.

Place a pink egg half on a paper plate. Add a cracker below the egg and top cracker with egg yolk mixture. Use carrot strips to make ropes. Use beets, ham and cheese strips to decorate balloon (see sketch).

½ pink-colored hard-boiled egg

ham strip

processed cheese strip

beet strip

carrot strips

soda or Triscuit cracker

egg-yolk mixture

Sky Giants Cupcake Cones

Materials Checklist

- ☐ 1 box cake mix
- ☐ 1 box flat-bottom ice cream cones (at least 10 cones)
- ☐ 1 can vanilla frosting
- ☐ food coloring in various colors
- ☐ colored sprinkles
- ☐ cookie sheet
- ☐ measuring cups
- ☐ small bowls
- ☐ mixing bowl
- ☐ mixing spoons
- ☐ electric beater
- ☐ plastic knives

Serves 10.

Preparation: Set out all materials so children can see ingredients. Have children wash and dry hands.

Procedure: Mix cake mix according to package directions. Fill ½ full 10 flat-bottom ice cream cones. Place on cookie sheet and bake at 350° for 25 minutes. While cupcake cones are baking, place vanilla frosting in small bowls, add food coloring to each and allow children to take turns stirring to mix.

Frost cupcake cones and sprinkle with colored sprinkles.

sprinkles

frosting

ice cream cone

Bubble Blow

Materials Checklist

☐ container of bubble solution for each team

☐ bubble-blowing wand for each team

☐ chalk

☐ paper

☐ pencil

☐ measuring tape

Preparation: With chalk, draw two lines, 20 feet (6 m) long and 10 feet (3 m) apart (see sketch). You may need to vary the distance between lines depending on the breeze.

Procedure: Divide group into two teams. Teams form two lines behind the starting line, with the breeze, if any, at their backs. Give the first player on each team a container of bubble solution and a bubble-blowing wand. Teacher stands at the finish line. When teacher says, "Go!" the first player on each team stands behind the starting line and blows one wand-full of bubbles toward the finish line. Players take turns blowing bubbles until everyone has had a turn or until time is up. With paper and pencil, teacher records how many bubbles from each team cross the finish line. Teams try to get as many bubbles as possible over the finish line.

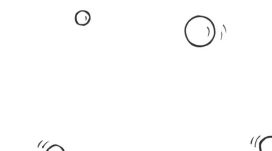

Balloon Kicker

Materials Checklist

☐ chalk or rope

☐ 5 balloons (or more)

☐ water

☐ pitcher

☐ large cardboard box

☐ measuring tape

Preparation: Pour approximately two tablespoons of water from pitcher into each balloon. (The water helps stabilize the balloons when they're being hit in the air.) Inflate balloons, tie them and put them in the box. Use chalk or rope to make a line 20 feet (6 m) long.

Procedure: Divide group into two teams. Team A plays on one side of the line and Team B plays on the other side. Team members spread out and get into crab positions (on hands and feet, backs to the ground, see sketch). If crab position is too difficult for children, they may play on their hands and knees. Teacher tosses a balloon to Team A. While staying in the crab position, a player on Team A uses a hand or foot to volley the balloon over the line to Team B. Teams volley the balloon back and forth as long as possible, using hands or feet. Players can move around, but they must stay in the crab position. When the balloon hits the ground, the teacher throws it back to the team that last hit the balloon. If the balloon pops, the teacher replaces it with one of the balloons in the box. (Keeping score as in volleyball is optional.)

Variation: Give a balloon to each team and see how many times they can hit the balloon before it touches the ground.

← 20 feet → (6 m)

Balloon Kisses

Materials Checklist

☐ balloons—one for every two children plus a few extras

☐ chalk or masking tape

☐ measuring tape

Preparation: Use chalk or masking tape to mark off two lines 30 to 40 feet (9 to 12 m) apart. Inflate balloons.

Procedure: Divide group into teams of four players. Each team then divides into two pairs. Give each pair a balloon. One pair in each team stands at one starting line and the other pair stands opposite their teammates on the other starting line. Partners stand side by side and link arms. When the teacher says, "Launch!" all the partners on both sides gently hit their balloons into the air with their free hands, trying to keep balloons up as they run toward their teammates. If the balloon drops to the ground they may pick it up, but must keep their arms linked. If the balloon pops, teacher provides a replacement. When each pair reaches their teammates, they continue to hit their balloons into the air to make their balloons touch. When the balloons touch, team shouts, "Balloon Kiss!" Pairs hold on to their balloons and run back to their starting places. Each pair then repeats process to accomplish two more balloon kisses, then they return to their starting positions and sit down. The first team with all members sitting wins.

Hot Air Ballooning Games•**Middler**

Updraft, Downdraft

Materials Checklist

☐ one inflated balloon for each team plus a few extras

Procedure: Divide class into two teams. Each team forms a line. First player in each line is given a balloon. When the balloonmeister (teacher) shouts, "Launch!" the first player shouts, "Updraft!" and hands the balloon over his or her head to the next player in line. The next player in line shouts, "Downdraft!" and hands the balloon through his or her legs to the next player in line. The balloon is passed in this alternating fashion to the last player. The last player shouts, "Deflate!" and sits on the balloon to pop it. As soon as the balloon pops the rest of the team sits down. The first team seated wins.

Hares and Hounds

Materials Checklist

☐ several colors of chalk

☐ balloons

☐ masking tape

Preparation: Make a starting line with chalk or masking tape. This game must be played on an open paved area such as a parking lot.

Procedure: (*Note:* A "Hares and Hounds" race is a common balloon festival event in which the "Hound" balloons follow one "Hare" balloon in an exciting chase.) Divide group into teams of five players. Each team lines up behind the starting line. Each team chooses a member to be a Hare. Each Hare is given a different color of chalk and a balloon. The Hares inflate their balloons without tying them. The rest of the team members are Hounds. Give each Hound a balloon to inflate and tie. When the balloonmeister

(teacher) says "Launch," the Hares let their balloons go. Wherever each Hare's balloon lands, he or she marks a number one on the pavement. The Hares continue inflating and releasing their balloons until they each have four numbers in their own color of chalk on the pavement. Then the Hare runs back to his or her team and tags the first Hound. The Hound volleys his or her balloon and steps on the number one made by his or her team's Hare. Hound repeats process for numbers two, three and four. The next Hound in line begins as soon as the previous Hound is moving toward number two. The balloonmeister watches carefully to make sure each hound steps on the correct numbers. (A Hound must keep volleying balloon in the air as he or she moves toward a number.) When each team member has completed this task he or she returns to the starting point and sits down. The first team to be sitting together wins.

X Marks the Spot

Materials Checklist

☐ chalk

☐ several balloons

☐ measuring tape

Preparation: Use chalk to draw two large circles about 15 feet (4.5 m) in diameter. Make a large *X* in the middle of each circle. Inflate balloons.

Procedure: Divide group into two teams. Each team sits inside one circle. Each team selects a balloonmeister's helper who stands outside the circle. Give helper a balloon and a piece of chalk. When the balloonmeister says, "Launch," each helper throws a balloon into team's circle. Team members shout, "Warm air," and, without standing up, use their feet and hands to keep the balloon in the air. When the balloon is over the *X*, team members shout, "Cool air," and let it fall.

If the balloon touches the *X*, the helper gives the team a point by making a chalk mark on the pavement. If the balloon falls anywhere else, the helper retrieves the balloon and throws it into the circle again. When the balloonmeister says, "Stop," the team with the most points wins.

15 feet (3.5 m)

Hot Air Ballooning Games • **Middler**

Kick the Cloud

Materials Checklist

☐ pillowcase

☐ balloons

☐ string

Preparation: Inflate balloons and tie ends. Fill pillowcase with balloons. Tie end of pillowcase with string.

Procedure: Children remove shoes. Have all but five or six children form a large circle on their knees. The remaining children then form a pinwheel formation in the center of the circle, lying on their backs, heads toward the center. The "cloud" (balloon-filled pillowcase) is then tossed into the circle. The object is for the children on their backs to kick or hit the cloud out of the circle, over the heads of the children in the outer circle. Children in the outer circle try to keep it in play. If the cloud is kicked over a player's head in the outer circle, that player joins the inner circle, exchanging places with the child who kicked it.

Hot Air Ballooning Games • Junior

Gondola Gallop

Materials Checklist

☐ four large appliance boxes

☐ craft knife

☐ chalk, masking tape or rope

☐ whistle

☐ measuring tape

Preparation: With chalk, masking tape or rope, draw four starting lines on opposite sides of an open area at least 20 yards (18 m) square. Cut out opposite sides of each box (see sketch).

Procedure: Divide group into four teams. Each team chooses a name for their balloon or gondola (High Flier, Way High, Zoomin' Balloon, Air Fair). Each team gathers at a starting line. Place a box by each starting line. Teacher acts as the balloonmeister (leader of the race). When balloonmeister blows the whistle, all team members get inside their "gondola" (box) and hold it up as they run to the opposite side of the playing area. At the opposite side all team members must disembark from their gondola, run around it five times, give a high five to each team member while saying, "Soft Landings," and get back into their gondola. Then the team runs back to its place. The first gondola to reach its starting place wins.

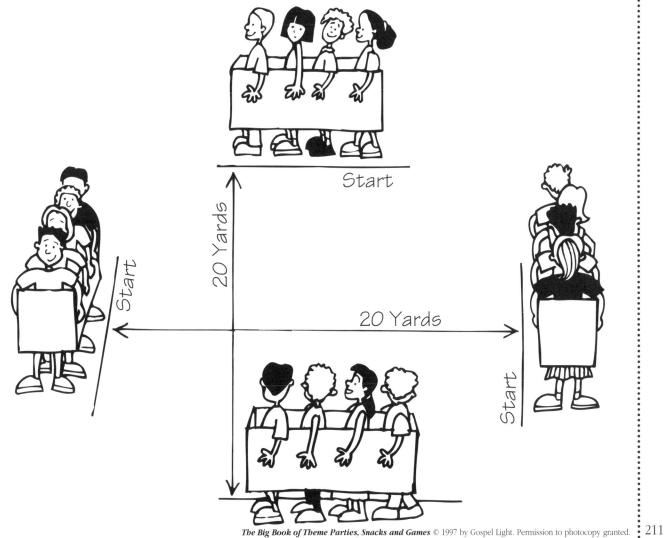

Hold the Ropes!

Materials Checklist

☐ one inflated balloon for each team, plus a few extras

☐ one 6-foot (1.8-m) rope for each team

☐ 8 chairs

☐ measuring tape

Preparation: Place four chairs in a line along one end of the playing area and four chairs in a line on the opposite side at least 40 feet (12 m) apart.

Procedure: Divide group into four teams. Each team forms a line behind a chair. First player in each line is given a balloon and a rope. When the teacher shouts, "Hold the ropes!" the first player on each team holds the balloon and the rope and runs around a chair at the opposite side, returning to his or her team. The first player hands the balloon to the second player. Then the first and second players, both holding the rope, run around the chair and back (see sketch).

The relay continues until the whole team is holding the rope, with the last player holding the balloon, as they run around the chair and back. If a player lets go of the rope or drops the balloon, the team has to return to the starting place and begin again. The first team to complete the relay wins.

Back to Balloons

Materials Checklist

☐ chalk, masking tape or rope

☐ several inflated balloons

☐ chair

Preparation: Make a starting line with chalk, masking tape or rope. Place a chair at the opposite side of the playing area.

Procedure: Divide group into two teams. Kids in each team group themselves into trios. (One or two kids may need to participate twice to even out the trios.) Both teams stand behind the starting line. The first trio on each team must stand back to back and lock arms. The teacher places a balloon between their backs (see sketch).

When the teacher says, "Launch!" the first trio on each team must go around the chair at the opposite side of the playing area and back to the starting line without dropping the balloon. Then the balloon is given to the next trio, who runs the relay following the same procedure as the first trio. The relay continues until each team member has participated. If a trio drops their balloon, they must start their leg of the relay again. The first team to finish wins.

All Together Now

Materials Checklist

☐ chalk, masking tape or rope

☐ several balloons

☐ measuring tape

Preparation: Make a start and finish line with chalk, masking tape or rope on the ground approximately 20 yards (18 m) apart. Inflate balloons.

Procedure: Divide group into two teams. Each team stands behind the starting line and makes a tight circle with their hands extended into the middle. Each team member grabs a hand of two other team members. The teacher places a balloon on the top of each team's grasped hands (see sketch).

When the teacher says, "Go!" each team runs to the finish line and back, keeping the balloon on top of their grasped hands. It is against the rules to wedge the balloon between arms. If a team lets the balloon drop, they must start over. The first team to complete the race wins.

Up and Away

Materials Checklist

☐ 10 balloons of equal shape and size

☐ 2 large containers (baskets or boxes)

☐ felt pen

Preparation: Inflate balloons. Write the numbers 1 through 10 on the balloons—one number on each balloon. Assign one container to each team.

Procedure: Divide group into two teams. Toss balloons in air. The object of the game is for the teams to get the higher-numbered balloons into their container without using their hands. Elbows, heads and feet may be used. The winning team is the one scoring the most points.

Index

Index

Smart Sunday School Helps

from Gospel Light

A ton of reproducible resources to help you recruit and motivate leaders and teachers, promote support within the congregation and increase attendance at Sunday School.

Advice, answers and articles on every aspect of teaching children. Reproducible so that you can give training to all of your teachers, volunteers and parents.

52 lively reproducible Bible-theme skits in each book. Each skit includes director's tips, Bible background information and group discussion questions. Less than 33¢ per skit!

Here's a great way to introduce Bible learning while the kids are busy with their crayons. *Bible Verse Coloring Pages* includes 116 verses in both NIV and KJV translations. These reproducible pages can be used again and again.

Here's a life-saving resource that puts the most current articles, tips, and quick solutions for teaching 5th and 6th graders at your fingertips. Use these reproducible pages for on-the-spot training or teacher refreshment. The perfect companion for any brand of curriculum.

Take the anxiety out of planning, staging and presenting programs for Advent, Christmas, Easter, Thanksgiving, Mother's Day and more. Includes 23 wide variety skits for all ages. Reproducible.

200 reproducible Bible learning games at your fingertips. Fun, active games for 1st through 6th graders that will help you review Bible stories, reinforce Bible memory verses and apply them to a child's life.

With this easy-to-use resource you'll be able to plan and put on the best parties for your kids! Get decorating ideas, clip art, fun snack recipes, great games and activities and much more! This resource works with all children's programs, including special events, day camps, Sunday School, VBS, Christian schools and home birthday parties.

Every word of these upbeat songs is straight from the Bible. It's the ultra-cool way to memorize the scriptures being studied in Gospel Light's 5th and 6th grade Sunday School curriculum, Planet 56! And it's reproducible–so you can make copies for all your kids.

These popular books include Bible verses, borders and hundreds of reproducible illustrations to help you create professional bulletins, flyers, posters and more. Complete with simple instructions.

Hand puppets grab your kids attention and help them remember your lesson. Use them at home, in Sunday School, VBS and anytime you want a child's full attention. *Easy-to-Make Puppets and How to Use Them* gives you great ideas to use puppets in the classroom and at home. Includes reproducible patterns and guidelines to make your job easier.

Crafts make ideal teaching activities. Each of these crafts include step-by-step instructions, illustrations and patterns using economical and easy-to-find materials.

These resources make record keeping simple and efficient. Each large, colorful Attendance Chart lets you keep track of your students for over two months. Give kids Peel 'n Press stickers so they can measure their weekly attendance!

Available through your local Christian Supplier   **Gospel Light**